Toolkit for Teachers of Literacy

Diane Hood Nettles

California University of Pennsylvania

PEARSON

Boston ▪ New York ▪ San Francisco
Mexico City ▪ Montreal ▪ Toronto ▪ London ▪ Madrid ▪ Munich ▪ Paris
Hong Kong ▪ Singapore ▪ Tokyo ▪ Cape Town ▪ Sydney

Executive Editor: Aurora Martinez Ramos
Senior Development Editor: Mary Kriener
Series Editorial Assistant: Lynda Giles
Executive Marketing Manager: Krista Clark
Composition and Prepress Buyer: Linda Cox
Manufacturing Buyer: Linda Morris
Manufacturing Manager: Megan Cochran
Cover Coordinator: Elena Sidorova
Editorial-Production Coordinator: Mary Beth Finch
Text Design and Electronic Composition: Denise Hoffman

For related titles and support materials, visit our online catalog at www.ablongman.com

Between the time Website information is gathered and then published, it is not unusual for some sites to have closed. Also, the transcription of URLs can result in unintended typographical errors. The publisher would appreciate notification where these errors occur so that they may be corrected in subsequent editions.

Library of Congress Cataloging-in-Publication Data not available at press time.

ISBN: 0-205-50414-0

Printed in the United States of America.

10 9 8 7 6 5 4 3 2 1   11 10 09 08 07 06

Contents

s e c t i o n   t w o

Rubrics for Analyzing Writing   35

section three

Reading Assessments for the Classroom Teacher   73

section four

Using Standards-Based Literacy Portfolios   93

s e c t i o n   f i v e

Phonics Mini-Lessons: Understanding the Nature of Words   121

Blackline Masters Available at www.ablongman.com/nettles

Introduction

Mrs. Pidgeon smiled. "I hear all sorts of interesting excuses for tardiness, but I have never heard that one before."

"I believe I'm unique," Gooney Bird said.

"Yes, you are, indeed."

■ *Gooney Bird Greene* (Lowry, 2002)

Did you ever wish you had a toolbox that you could keep in your desk drawer, and in it would be every tool imaginable to cope with anything your students handed you? When a situation in the classroom presented itself, all you'd have to do is open the drawer, pull out the box, find the right tool, and *voila!* Your problem is solved.

Ah, but toolboxes just aren't that big. Every unique situation, every Gooney Bird Greene, every learning need, requires the teacher's thoughtful attention. Good teachers know that the key to their successful classroom experiences and ultimately the key to their students' learning is their own ability to connect personally with their students, and to realize the unique needs of each one. That takes insightful reflection, and more than just pulling tools out of a box.

But good teachers also know that there are some teaching tools and strategies that work well. When students are engaged, when they are asked to think, and when they are personally invested in the task, they learn. Such tools and strategies, used thoughtfully by the teacher, can facilitate literacy understanding.

That is the purpose of this book. In five sections, I offer some tools that will help you meet the literacy needs of your students. But these tools are not the type you simply pull out of the box and reproduce. These are tools that can be adapted, altered, and rearranged in many ways, to help your students become invested in their learning of reading and writing skills. These tools require you to make decisions, think beyond the script of the basal teacher's edition, and use your teaching talents to bring out the best in your students.

In Section One, you'll see "Teaching Tools for Reading Instruction," which offers you a set of teaching strategies, graphic organizers, classroom management tips, and assessments that you can use to meet a variety of needs, including early literacy, standards-based teaching, and use of technology.

Writing assessments comprise Section Two. Called "Rubrics for Analyzing Writing," this section offers a set of rubrics that are based on Vicki Spandel's Six Traits Writing Model. I've adapted the six traits to align with commonly used state writing standards, and included benchmarks for grades 1–5, as well as a set of rubrics for middle school writers.

Section Three, called "Reading Assessments for the Classroom Teacher," is a set of assessment tools and forms to use in determining your students' reading abilities. All of the assessments in this section can be done quickly, with students reading aloud to you in private one-to-one sessions. You can discover a myriad of reading abilities in this adaptation of Marie Clay's running record format, including the reader-text match, as well as the student's use of word clues from the print, comprehension of the selection through retelling, and ability to read fluently and with appropriate speed. The tools can be tailored to your time constraints and needs; all of the reading behaviors can be assessed, using a comprehensive assessment form, or you can use mini-assessments and determine just one reading ability at a time.

Section Four, titled "Using Standards-Based Literacy Portfolios," is a comprehensive look at the use of portfolios in assessing your students' literacy abilities. I define literacy portfolios, and then show you some of the possibilities for your students' literacy portfolios.

In this section, there are seven areas that I recommend for documentation, which include four of the areas of reading instruction required by the No Child Left Behind Act: phonics, vocabulary, comprehension, and fluency. Also included are ways to use the portfolio to document your students' personal reading and writing. In each of these crucial areas of literacy development, I will describe some ways that you can help your students document their abilities, and offer a student checklist for inclusion in the portfolio.

In this era of standards-based education and emphasis on the "basics" of word-attack skills, you may be feeling the need for a little refresher course in phonics. If so, then Section Five, "Phonics Mini-Lessons," is for you. This is a set of fifteen quick and simple lessons that you can use to relearn the terms, elements, and generalizations of phonics. Teachers need to know the "lingo" of their profession and of the content they must teach. This section gives you that.

Many of the figures and worksheets in the Toolkit are large enough to be copied or can be recreated for your own use in the classroom. That is an important purpose of this book—to give you the tools you need in the classroom. In addition, you can also find the blackline masters for many of the forms and organizers provided in Sections One, Three, and Four online at www.ablongman.com/nettles. I hope you find them helpful.

In conclusion, this Toolkit is yours to use as any good teacher would—to solve problems in the classroom, to enhance student learning, to engage students in thoughtful application of strategies, and to advance your own knowledge. While I cannot offer instant solutions to the unique challenges of every classroom, I can offer some support, some tried-and-true strategies, and a good place to start. Enjoy, and go teach!

Teaching Tools for Reading Instruction

> For fifty-seven years my great-aunt Arizona hugged her students. She hugged them when their work was good, and she hugged them when it was not. She taught them words and numbers, and about the faraway places they would visit someday.
>
> "Have you been there?" the students asked.
>
> "Only in my mind," she answered. "But someday you will go."
>
> ■ *My Great Aunt Arizona* (Houston, 1992)

To take your students to faraway places, there is no better way than to read, read, and read some more. This section of the *Toolkit* offers you a myriad of strategies, tools, and ideas that you can use in your classroom in a variety of ways to facilitate your students' comprehension of what they read and to help make your classroom a place where learning is valued. You'll see various tips and teaching strategies organized around five common themes in literacy instruction: early literacy, ways to work with story elements, tools for understanding nonfiction, comprehension and critical reading strategies, and classroom management ideas.

Early Literacy Tools

Is there anything more exciting than watching very young children realize their reading abilities? Two simple tools for assessing early literacy are offered on the following pages, and both of them allow you to watch children as they grow with print. They can be used on an on-going basis, and are designed to be used quickly, in one-on-one sessions with children who are just beginning to learn to read. Additionally, I have included some activities for allowing young children build upon what they know about environmental print.

■ Alphabet Recognition Checklist

Why is it necessary for children to recognize the alphabet? Conventional wisdom aside, the interesting thing about alphabet knowledge is that a youngster truly does not need to know the names of the letters in our English alphabet in order to read. It is quite possible for a child to see the written word, "dog," and say its verbal equivalent. The child would not need to be able to tell you that the first written symbol in this word is the letter "d." As long as he can make the sound represented by this little scribble on the page, it really doesn't matter whether or not he can say "dee" when you point to the "d" and ask him to identify it. However, when conversing with others about the mechanics of reading, children must know the names to call all of these written symbols on the page. It is most helpful for a five-year-old to know which one of the symbols in the word "dog" is the "d."

Thus, an alphabet recognition checklist is helpful. Shown in Figures 1.1, 1.2, and 1.3 are a checklist that I have adapted, along with the student pages. Notice that there are two different sets of student pages, printed in different fonts. Some teachers find it useful to assess a child's ability to recognize the alphabet as it is printed in different type fonts, because certain letters, such as the "a" and the "g," are reproduced differently, depending on the font. Sometimes children become confused with the differences in appearance of these letters.

Figure 1.1 ■ Alphabet Recognition Checklist

Child's Name	Names the Letter		Writes the Letter	
	Upper Case	Lower Case	Upper Case	Lower Case
Aa				
Bb				
Cc				
Dd				
Ee				
Ff				
Gg				
Hh				
Ii				
Jj				
Kk				
Ll				
Mm				
Nn				
Oo				
Pp				
Qq				
Rr				
Ss				
Tt				
Uu				
Vv				
Ww				
Xx				
Yy				
Zz				

Figure 1.2 ■ Student Lower Case Alphabet
Recognition Sheet

w	f	r	t	s	a	m
q	y	o	z	b	c	x
n	l	i	j	e	v	h
d	g	p	u	k		
w	f	r	t	s	a	m
q	y	o	z	b	c	x
n	l	i	j	e	v	h
d	g	p	u	k		

Figure 1.3 ■ Student Upper Case Alphabet
Recognition Sheet

W	F	R	T	S	A	M
Q	Y	O	Z	B	C	X
N	L	I	J	E	V	H
D	G	P	U	K		
W	F	R	T	S	A	M
Q	Y	O	Z	B	C	X
N	L	I	J	E	V	H
D	G	P	U	K		

Also notice that the assessment contains two components: naming and writing. You can use this checklist to record how well the child can verbally name letters of the alphabet, as well as how well he or she can reproduce the letters in writing. This checklist assesses recognition and generation of letters; it does not, however, assess letter-sound recognition.

Directions:

1. Have available the Upper Case Alphabet Recognition Sheet and some lined writing paper. Ask the child to write his or her name on the lined paper.

2. Present the Upper Case Alphabet Recognition Sheet in the font of your choice. Point to the first letter and ask the child to name it.

3. Then, using some lined writing paper, ask the child to write the letter.

4. Repeat the procedure for each of the letters on the recognition sheet. Be sure to stay in the same order as shown on the sheet; do not present the alphabet in its usual sequence.

5. Repeat the assessment using the Lower Case Alphabet Recognition Sheet in the font of your choice.

■ Reading Awareness Checklist for Young Children

Very young children often surprise teachers and caregivers with their knowledge of concepts about print and reading. Exposure to all types of media, personal experiences, and familiarity with books gives young children many skills in handling print. The checklist shown in Figure 1.4 can help you determine what your youngest students know about reading. Use the list over a period of time to record the date when you first observe the student's behavior. The list can be used repeatedly, by giving the child a picture book and asking him or her to "share this book with me."

Figure 1.4 ■ Reading Awareness Checklist for Young Children

Reading Awareness Description	Comments and Date
1. The child demonstrates understanding that a book holds meaning.	
2. The child treats a book differently from the way he treats another object, such as a toy.	
3. The child holds the book right side up.	
4. The child turns to the beginning of the book.	
5. The child begins sharing a book on the first page.	
6. The child moves from left to right through the book.	
7. The child moves from left to right on the page.	
8. The child moves across the page and down to the left, moving down the page.	
9. The child "keeps place" with his finger or some other method of marking.	
10. The child uses pictures to read or tell the text.	
11. The child matches individually spoken words with the individual written words in the text.	
12. The child's verbal story or retelling matches the written text.	
13. The child uses "book language" to tell or read the text.	
14. The child phonetically decodes words: most some none	
15. The child can, when asked, point to individual words.	
16. The child can, when asked, point to the beginning of a word on the page.	
17. The child can, when asked, point to the end of a word on the page.	
18. The child can, when asked, point to the middle of a word on the page.	
19. The child can, when asked, point to the beginning of a sentence on the page.	
20. The child can, when asked, point to the end of a sentence on the page.	

■ Environmental Print

Environmental print is the kind of print that surrounds us everyday: Burger King®, Wal-mart®, and Coca-Cola® are a few words that your students may see in their neighborhoods or even at school. These are the words that children recognize before any others because they are part of their surroundings; these words often take on meaning before any others do. While Yaden, Rowe, and MacGillivray (2000) report that experimental studies do not show strong support for depending upon environmental print to help children develop reading abilities, this type of print is highly recognizable; often associated with things that are important and familiar to them; and can be motivating for young children. Moreover, environmental print can be used to create text that provides the "conventional" reading experiences that Yaden and others have found to be most useful (p. 439). Thus, environmental print can be used in strategies in which students need to use words they already know to create new words or provide text that they can read.

Logo Scrapbooks.   Cut out logos from familiar items such as cereal boxes, labels from toys, can labels, old paper menus, boxes such as McDonald's French fries, and so on. Put these in a scrapbook or magnetic page photo album. Children like to find words and logos that they recognize. Have them dictate sentences about the places where they have been. Make up stories or narratives that use these sentences, and create books for children to read.

Photograph Albums.   After taking pictures of classroom activities, put them in a photo album. Label them with captions that the children dictate. You can also ask the children to bring in baby pictures and other photographs from home, and create individual albums with captioned pictures, or a class album of "When We Were Very Young."

Classroom Labels in Sentences.   Many early childhood teachers label objects in the classroom, so that students can see words like *desk, chair, chalkboard,* and *clock.* Go one step further and use labels that show a complete sentence, such as, "This is a <u>chair</u>," or "This is the <u>clock</u>." Underline or put a box around the target word. Create books that describe students and events in the classroom, using these words and photographs to illustrate. Here is one example:

> Mara sits in a chair. Her chair is by the clock.
>
> Pedro sits in a chair. His chair is by the door.
>
> Lu sits in a chair. His chair is by the window.

Charts and Classroom Directions.   Wherever possible, put your organizational techniques in writing. Create charts that help students know their classroom jobs, or where items belong. Create lists such as the daily schedule, attendance records, or group arrangements. Give the students opportunities to read and find out these housekeeping types of things for themselves.

Strategies for Facilitating Work with Story Elements

When a good reader reads fiction, he or she knows what to expect of a story. The reader knows that stories consist of character, setting, plot, and theme. While reading, if something is missing, or underdeveloped, his or her sense of equilibrium with that story becomes unbalanced. Metacognitive abilities kick in, and the reader begins to search for clues to understanding the story. You can enable your readers' comprehension of stories by explicitly teaching the story elements, using children's literature titles that have strong elements in them.

In this section, you'll see ways to use story maps, which are graphic representations of the elements of story. Story maps are extremely popular these days. You'll see how to help students sequence events in a story, how to help students pick out story elements, as well as some book lists of excellent titles to use for this purpose.

■ Story Maps

If you've ever used a story map with your students, you know that it is a visual representation of a story, in which the reader jots down the basic elements of the story: character, setting, plot, and resolution. A simple story map might look like the one shown in Figure 1.5.

There are many ways to vary a story map. Because there are usually five elements, teachers sometimes ask students to trace a hand and put an element on each finger. Or, they reproduce a large picture of a star and ask students to write an element on each point. Listed below are several websites that contain information about story maps; most include downloadable maps.

Figure 1.5 ■ Story Map

Setting	Place: Time:
Characters	
Problem	
Resolution	
Theme	

- Enchanted Learning. (1996). Enchanted learning graphic organizers. Retrieved April 10, 2006, form http://www.enchantedlearning.com/graphicorganizers/star/
- Fry, P. (2001). Story maps and boxes. In *Education World teacher lesson plans.* Retrieved February 27, 2006, from http://www.education-world.com/a_tsl/TM/WS_storymapws.shtml
- Jones, R. (2001). History frames/story maps. In *ReadingQuest.org: Making sense in the social studies.* Retrieved February 27, 2006, from http://curry.edschool.virginia.edu/go/readquest/strat/storymaps.html
- Read Write Think. (2002). Story mapping. Retrieved April 10, 2006, from http://www.readwritethink.org/materials/storymap/index.html
- Scholastic. (1996). Scholastic teachers graphic organizers. Retrieved April 10, 2006, from http://teacher.scholastic.com/lessonplans/graphicorg/

Figure 1.6 ■ Ways to Use Story Maps

Before Reading	During Reading	After Reading
• Show a blank map, ask students to make predictions about story elements. • Give students a list of vocabulary and a blank map. Insert words in logical places on the map. • Show items from a book box that depict elements of the story. Have students fill in a story map to outline a "mind movie" of the story, based on the clues given with the objects. • Cut the story apart. Give each group a piece of the story (usually one page). Using a blank story map, determine which element is most reflected in the story piece.	• Keep the story map handy to look for elements as students read. • Fill out a map before reading with predictions, and then change the predictions to actual events as students read. • Cut the story map apart. Give each student or group a piece of the map. As they read, they must look for their portion of the story. After reading, everyone shares what they found out.	• Give students a blank map and have them fill it in as they recall events and elements. • Keep copies of story maps filled in after reading several stories. Cut the maps apart. Create a new story by borrowing pieces of each story map. • Use the story map to verbally retell the story. • Use the story map to write a retelling of the story.

Story maps can be used in a multitude of ways. To facilitate understanding and use of predictions, use them before reading. Used during reading, story maps can aid in metacognitive comprehension, as they remind students of things to look for as they read. And, used after reading, story maps can serve as assessment tools for your students' comprehension. Shown in Figure 1.6 is a chart that outlines ways to use story maps.

■ Sequencing Events in a Story

To facilitate understanding of a story, it is often helpful to ask the student to retell the events in the story, in the **sequence** in which they occurred. You can give them a scaffold for this by indicating the number of events needed in the retelling, or by providing a sequential map that helps them place the events in order, such as the one shown in Figure 1.7. You can use long rectangular pieces of newsprint, and ask students to fold the paper in half, then in half again, to create four squares. For eight events, fold one more time. You can also have them fold in thirds. This is a quick, easy way to produce a story map, and it does not require use of the copy machine. Students can write or draw the events in sequential order. Help them look for words the author uses to signal the events, such as "first," "next," "last," "finally," and "after."

Figure 1.7 ■ A Sequential Map

First	Next	Then	Last

Figure 1.8 ■ A B-M-E Map

Beginning	**Middle**	**End**

Very young children can begin to understand the order of events in a story by using a "B-M-E Map," which shows events at the beginning, middle, and end of the story, as in Figure 1.8.

■ Character Analysis

Characters are often the reason we return again and again to certain books. We care about characters in some books because the authors have done such a good job of creating them that they seem like real people—people with whom we can identify.

In order to fully appreciate and understand fiction, your students will need to be able to explain why characters do the things they do, or describe the traits of the character that affect the outcome of the story. Story frames that focus on characters can help, because they require the student to determine the importance of the character and his or her actions. Shown here are two such frames; Figure 1.9 analyzes the main character of the story, and Figure 1.10 compares two characters.

Figure 1.9 ■ Character Analysis Story Frame

> **Title:** _____
>
> **Author:** _____
>
> _____ is an important character in this story, because
> _____.
>
> He/She wanted _____, but
> _____.
>
> So, he/she_____.
>
> I think that_____ is _____, because
> _____.

Suggested books with strong characters, for use with this frame:

Picture Books

Adventures of Pippi Longstocking (Lindgren, 1997)
Amazing Grace (Hoffman, 1991)
Amelia Bedelia and the Baby (Parish, 1981)
Chrysanthemum (Henkes, 1991)
Moses Goes to School (Millman, 2000)
My Name is Yoon (Recorvits, 2003)
Suki's Kimono (Uegaki, 2003)
Tacky the Penguin (Lester, 1988)
Thank You, Mr. Falker (Polacco, 1998)
Tom (dePaola, 1993)

Chapter Books

Ramona Quimby, Age 8 (Cleary, 1981)
Sahara Special (Codell, 2003)
Stargirl (Spinelli, 2000)

Figure 1.10 ■ Character Comparison Story Frame

Title: _____

Author: _____

_____ and _____ are two characters in this story.

_____ is _____,

but _____ is _____.

I know this because _____

_____.

Suggested books for use with the character comparison frame:

Picture Books

Arthur's Teacher Trouble (Brown, 1986)
George and Martha Back in Town (Marshall, 1984)
Pink and Say (Pollacco, 1994)
Hey Al (Yorinks, 1988)
Tops and Bottoms (Stevens, 1995)

Chapter Books

Charlotte's Web (White, 1952)
Double Fudge (Blume, 2002)
Silent to the Bone (Konigsburg, 2000)

■ Plot Analysis

The way to understanding a story is through its **plot**. The plot, which consists of the characters' problem and their attempts to solve it, is the "meat" of the story, and the essence of the author's message. Students need to be able to pick out the problem in the story, and determine how the author chose to allow the characters to solve it. Many times, there are multiple attempts to solve the problem, giving the story twists and turns that provide interest.

Students can use clues to help them determine the plot from the author's words, from pictures, and from their own experiences. The author will provide hints to the problem by using words that connote difficulty, or words that have a negative tone. The illustrations, if there are any, also can offer clues about the problem, indicating discord, unhappiness, or struggle. These clues and hints can be combined with the reader's own experiences that are similar to the ones presented in the story. Such experiences help the reader surmise the problem that the author portrays.

Once the problem is determined, the reader can figure out the conflict. There are several types of conflicts, shown below:

- Conflict between the character and other characters (Example: Nick and his teacher in *Frindle* by Andrew Clements, 1996)
- Conflict between the character and nature (Example: Brian and winter in *Brian's Winter* by Gary Paulsen, 1996)
- Conflict within the character (Example: Unhei, a girl from Korea who must decide what her American name will be, in *The Name Jar* by Yangsook Choi, 2001)

Figure 1.11 ■ A Story Frame for Identifying Plot

Title: _____

Author: _____

In this story, the problem begins when _____

_____ .

This problem is one that is between the main character and _____ .

First, the character tries to solve it by _____ .

After that, _____ .

Then, _____ .

The problem is solved when _____

_____ .

At the end, _____ .

Books that have strong problems and can be used to analyze plots are:

Picture Books

The Frog Prince Continued (Scieszka, 1991)
Ira Sleeps Over (Waber, 1972)
Jingle Bells, Homework Smells (de Groat, 2000)
The Little Old Lady Who Was Not Afraid of Anything (Williams, 1986)
The Mighty Asparagus (Radunsky, 2004)
The Name Jar (Choi, 2001)
The _Old Man and His Door_ (Soto, 1996)
Sylvester and the Magic Pebble (Steig, 1969)
Too Many Tamales (Soto, 1993)

Chapter Books

The Beast in Ms. Rooney's Room (Giff, 1984)
Brian's Winter (Paulsen, 1996)
The Cheat (Koss, 2003)
Dear Whiskers (Nagda, 2000)
A Dog Called Kitty (Wallace, 1980)
Freckle Juice (Blume, 1971)
Frindle (Clements, 1996)
Holes (Sachar, 1998)
James and the Giant Peach (Dahl, 1961)
The Mouse and the Motorcycle (Cleary, 1965)
The Star of Kazan (Ibbotson, 2004)
Surviving the Applewhites (Tolan, 2002)

Once your students have read and thought about the problem in a story, they can represent it in a story frame, such as the one shown in Figure 1.11.

■ Setting Analysis

An often overlooked story element is the **setting**, yet it can be the key to understanding the author's message. Historical fiction is particularly dependent on the time and place of the story, and often, a reader's background knowledge of the historical context is insufficient to fully understand the story. Thus, you would need to facilitate identification of the setting. Additionally, some stories have multiple settings, and the plot moves around as the time and place changes. Young readers need to be able to identify the settings and their impact on the story.

Have your students look for dates, times, and places. Sometimes pictures will be the only clues; other times, the author will introduce the setting in words. When reading aloud to even your youngest readers, get into the habit of talking about setting right away. As you introduce a book, let the setting be part of your conversation. Moreover, have students use a story frame like the ones shown in Figures 1.12 and 1.13 to record information about settings.

Figure 1.12 ■ A Story Frame for Identifying Setting

> Title: _____
>
> Author: _____
>
> The time of this story is _____ .
>
> I know this because the author says, "_____
>
> _____ ."
>
> The place of this story is _____ .
>
> I know this because the author says, "_____
>
> _____ ."

Suggested books to use with the Setting Story Frame:

The Butterfly (Polacco, 2000)
Cheyenne Again (Bunting, 1995a)
The Color of Home (Hoffman, 2002)
Gleam and Glow (Bunting, 2001)

Nothing Ever Happens on 90th Street (Schotter, 1999)
So Far from the Sea (Bunting, 1998)

Figure 1.13 ■ A Story Frame for Identifying Multiple Settings in a Story

> Title: _____
>
> Author: _____
>
> This story has more than one setting. At the beginning, the place of this story is _____
>
> _____ .
>
> The time at the beginning is _____ .
>
> Later, the place of the story is _____ , and the time is
>
> _____ .
>
> This is important because _____
>
> _____ .

Suggested books to use with the Multiple Settings Story Frame:

Arthur Meets the President (Brown, 1991)
Dandelions (Bunting, 1995b)
Horton Hatches the Egg (Seuss, 1940)
Make Way for Ducklings (McCloskey, 1941)

Rosie's Walk (Hutchins, 1968)
This Is the Place for Me (Cole, 1986)
Where the Wild Things Are (Sendak, 1963)

■ Theme Analysis

Often, the author has a message to impart to readers. This message is the author's purpose for writing the story, and usually nudges the reader toward a basic truth about life. Such a message in a story is the **theme**. Many children have difficulty comprehending the author's theme because it is only implied and depends upon the child's ability to infer information that is not explicitly stated. It also depends on the child's past experiences and ability to apply them to what he reads. As Rosenblatt (1978) tells us in her description of the transactional theory, each of us can draw a different conclusion from the same story, based on our unique experiences. To help students determine the author's implied message or theme, ask questions such as: "Why did the author write this book?" or "How can this book help us understand things that happen to us in our lives?" Additionally, have them use the story frame in Figure 1.14, which helps them justify their theme choices.

Figure 1.14 ■ A Theme Story Frame

```
      Title: _____

      Author: _____

   In this story, the author seems to be giving me a message. In one sentence, this is the

   message: _____ .

   One reason I decided on this theme is _____

   _____

   _____ .

   Another reason I decided on this theme is _____

   _____

   _____ .

   This theme helps me in my everyday life because _____

   _____

   _____ .
```

Suggested books to use with the Theme Story Frame:

Picture Books

The Alphabet Tree (Lionni, 1968)
Fables (Lobel, 1980)
Hey, Al (Yorinks, 1986)
The Leaving Morning (Johnson, 1992)
Pink and Say (Polacco, 1994)
The Rebellious Alphabet (Diaz, 1993)
Swimmy (Lionni, 1963)
Suki's Kimono (Uegaki, 2003)
Thank You, Mr. Falker (Polacco, 1998)
Too Much Noise (McGovern, 1967)

Chapter Books

Before We Were Free (Alvarez, 2002)
Charlotte's Web (White, 1952)
Because of Winn Dixie (DiCamillo, 2000)
Is My Friend at Home? Pueblo Fireside Tales
    (Bierhorst, 2001)
A Jar of Dreams (Uchida, 1981)
The Secret School (Avi, 2001)
Stargirl (Spinelli, 2000)
Why Do They Hate Me? (Holliday, 1999)
Year of Impossible Goodbyes
    (Choi, 1991)

Strategies for Facilitating Work with Nonfiction Text

Over the years, so many of my students, from first grade to the college level, have wrinkled their noses when told to read for information. There are specialized skills necessary to read nonfiction, which many students never cultivate as well as the skills they need to enjoy a story. Moreover, informational, or expository, text differs from fiction. It contains difficult vocabulary, and many times, children have not developed schemata for the concepts behind the words (Anderson, 2004; Anderson & Pearson, 1984; Rumelhart, 1980). Pages are busier, containing graphs, charts, tables, and photographs with captions, which children sometimes find difficult to navigate. Features such as the index, table of contents, and the headings require special skills (Dreher, 2002). Additionally, much of the nonfiction that your students will read is electronic. The features of electronic text, such as additional links, animated graphics, and colorful fonts, can be distracting, especially to struggling readers. Reading and comprehending these visuals requires focus and skill that aren't necessarily the same as those for reading traditional text (Leu, 2002; Moss, 2004).

However, nonfiction provides a wealth of information, and children love to read about things that interest them (Palmer & Stewart, 2003). Many times, reluctant readers will attempt nonfiction because the topic is motivating to them. Additionally, many of the reading passages on standardized tests are nonfiction passages (Calkins, Montgomery, Santman, & Falk, 1998), and most state standards reflect the need to read nonfiction (Kletzien & Dreher, 2004).

Nonfiction authors often organize their writing in one of five patterns: descriptive, sequential, comparison, cause/effect, and problem/solution. Just as it is helpful to know about story elements in fiction, it is also helpful to know about nonfiction text structures. Students who have schemata for the way in which the text is laid out will know what to expect as they read; they will also be better able to look for information. For example, if the student knows that a piece of text has comparison structure, then he or she will look for ways that the author compares one topic to another. This leads the student to the author's main ideas.

Graphic organizers that illustrate text structure are very helpful for this. Some teachers will familiarize their students with text structure and their corresponding organizers. Then, when they encounter a new piece of text, all that is necessary is to show the students a blank organizer. Immediately, the students know the structure of the text and the types of things they'll need to look for (Villaume & Brabham, 2001). After filling in an organizer, they can write about the main ideas, using a frame that guides them. Eventually, students can work without the frame. On the following pages, common organizers that can be used for each of the five text structures are shown and discussed: descriptive, sequential, comparison, cause/effect, and problem/solution.

■ Descriptive Nonfiction Text Structure

When your students need to determine the main ideas of nonfiction text, it helps to ask them to look for a specific number of ideas. This is where a web organizer such as the one shown in Figure 1.15 can help. If the author has written in such a way that

Figure 1.15 ■ Web Organizer for Use with Descriptive Informational Text

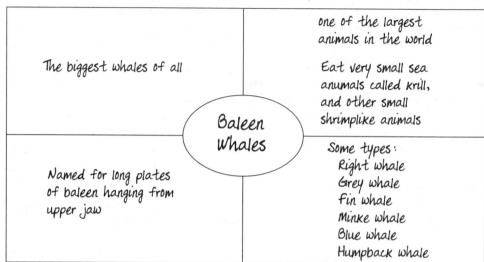

clearly describes the topic within four or more points, use the graphic organizer shown above, adjusting the number of main ideas needed by drawing diagonal lines from the center to the four corners of the square. Or, you can remove the outer frames of the square, and use only as many "spokes" on the circle as you need for main ideas. Signal words to look for in descriptive text are words that signify color, size, shape, habitat, and location. The map in Figure 1.15 was completed after reading *Whales* by Seymour Simon (1989).

Once your students have mapped the information on the web, they can write about it, using a frame like the one shown in Figure 1.16. Your goal is for them to develop the ability to write summaries on their own, without the frame.

Figure 1.16 ■ Report Frame for Descriptive Informational Text

Title: _Whales_

Author: _Seymour Simon_

In this book, the author tells about _baleen whales_ .

I found out _four_ new facts about _baleen whales_ . These facts are:

Baleen whales are the biggest of all the whales, and are named for long

plates hanging from the upper jaw. They eat krill, which are small

animals that look like shrimp. Some baleen whales are the right whale,

the grey whale, the minke whale, and the humpback whale. There are

many other types.

■ Sequential Nonfiction Text Structure

Nonfiction text also often contains a sequence, such as when authors of how-to books describe steps in a procedure. Ask students to list the steps in a chart like the one in Figure 1.17, adjusting it for the number of important steps listed in the text. If the author listed many more steps than you want your students to remember, you can list page numbers or key words to help them determine which steps should be listed.

For books that outline important historical events or biographies, the two charts in Figure 1.18 work best for ordering chronological events. Be sure to select a book that clearly has four major events to put in the chronology. If the book is a biography, ask students to choose one important timeframe in the person's life, such as his/her childhood, involvement in a war or political event, term in office, or other highly identifiable set of events. You can give them a range of page numbers with which to work, or give them a choice of time frames from which to choose. Students can draw and/or list the events in the boxes; they should list the dates in the second chart.

Your students can write about sequentially ordered events using the report frame shown in Figure 1.19.

Figure 1.17 ■ Identifying Sequential Steps

Steps in a Procedure
1.
2.
3.
4.
5.
6.

Figure 1.18 ■ Charts for Chronological Events

Chart without Dates

First Event	Second Event	Third Event	Fourth Event

Chart with Dates

Date:	Date:	Date:	Date:	Date:

Figure 1.19 ■ Report Frame for Sequentially Ordered Text

Title: _____

Author: _____

In this book, I learned _____ .

First, _____

_____ .

Second, _____

_____ .

Third, _____

_____ .

Finally, _____

_____ .

■ Cause-Effect Nonfiction Text Structure

One of the most difficult conclusions for children to draw from nonfiction text is that of the cause/effect relationship. Many authors write about historical events, which are part of a chain reaction of causes and effects. Other topics, such as animal behavior, the environment, economics, and weather have cause/effect relationships. Tell students to look for cause/effect relationships in texts that focus on these topics. While signal words can help (such words include *because, if, then, why, purpose, what happens, cause, effect, as a result, caused by, resulting from,* and *produces*), children often still have difficulty seeing the cause and effect.

Graphic organizers like the ones shown in Figure 1.20 can help students sort out the information. Sometimes, there is more than one effect; thus, the organizer needs multiple spaces for information.

Figure 1.20 ■ Sample Cause-Effect Graphic Organizers

Cause   Effect

Cause   Effect #1   Effect #2

Cause:

Here is what happened: _____

_____

_____

This caused these results:

Effect #1	Effect #2	Effect #3

Many times, the author states the effect before stating the cause! For example, look at this passage, from Simon's *Animals Nobody Loves* (2001):

> The bubonic plague, or "Black Death," was spread by flea-infested rats during the 1300's. More than 25 million deaths were caused by this disease—one third of the entire population of Europe at that time.

Therefore, it can be helpful to tell students to first look for the end result, or the effect. You can facilitate that by asking students to read, and then retell what they found out. Ask them to find out the answer to this question: "What happened, from beginning to end?"

In this case, students should determine the following:

> In the 1300's, flea-infested rats spread the bubonic plague, so 25 million people died.

Write this sequence of events for them, and ask, "What was the end result?" Students should point to the fact that 25 million people died. This end result is the effect. By using a cause/effect graphic organizer, as shown in Figure 1.21, you can help your students visualize the relationship. Write the students' "effect" on the chart.

Then, ask, "Why did that happen?" They'll need to find events that lead up to this final effect. In the example shown in Figure 1.22, the author tells us that flea-infested rats spread the bubonic plague.

Students can also use report frames like the one shown in Figure 1.23, which give them a scaffold for organizing cause/effect relationships in writing.

Figure 1.21

25 million deaths in Europe

Cause   Effect

Figure 1.22

Flea-infested rats spread the bubonic plague

25 million deaths in Europe

Cause   Effect

Figure 1.23 ■ Report Frame for Organizing Cause/Effect Relationships

Title: _____

Author: _____

The author of this book tells what happens when _____ .

I learned that if _____ , then _____

_____ .

After that, if _____ , then _____

_____ .

■ Compare/Contrast Relationships in Nonfiction Text

Students are often expected to find compare/contrast relationships when they read nonfiction, or to compare two entities when they write. Comparison writing patterns are common in nonfiction books about animals, plants, astronomy, simple machines, and geography, among other topics. Authors also use this type of pattern when explaining how our ancestors lived, comparing their lives to ours in modern times. Words often used by these authors include: *different, alike, same, compare, share,* and *common.*

If two topics are being compared, and the second topic is one that is well known to the reader, the comparison allows him or her to add to what the person already knows, which is reflective of the way children learn. For example, an author who describes wolves can point out the similarities and differences that wolves have to dogs, which are more likely to be familiar to children.

When the text is of comparison text structure, you can enhance your students' comprehension of it with an organizer that shows similarities and differences between the two topics. A Venn Diagram is one simple and popular way to accomplish this (see Figure 1.24). Attributes unique to each of the topics are written in the large circles; similarities are written in the intersection. This example was completed while reading *All About Frogs* by Jim Arnoskey (2002).

Another way to record information from comparison text is the two-sided chart, shown in Figure 1.25, which allows more room for writing facts.

Figure 1.24 ■ Venn Diagram

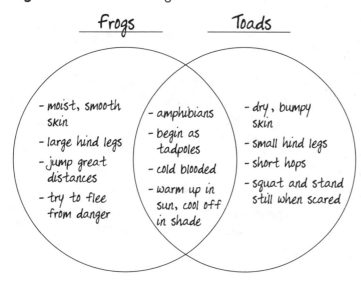

Frogs / Toads

- moist, smooth skin
- large hind legs
- jump great distances
- try to flee from danger

- amphibians
- begin as tadpoles
- cold blooded
- warm up in sun, cool off in shade

- dry, bumpy skin
- small hind legs
- short hops
- squat and stand still when scared

Figure 1.25 ■ Two-Sided Comparison Chart

Topic #1: _____	Topic #2: _____
How They Are Alike	**How They Are Different**

Figure 1.26 ■ Report Frame for Summarizing Comparative Text

Title: _____

Author: _____

The author of this book compares _____ to _____ .

They are alike in many ways. First, _____
_____ .

Second, _____
_____ .

Third, _____
_____ .

They are different in many ways. First, _____
_____ .

Second, _____
_____ .

Third, _____
_____ .

In conclusion, _____ .

After they have collected information and organized it, use the report frame in Figure 1.26 to help students write a summary of text that compares.

■ Problem/Solution Nonfiction Text Structure

Understanding nonfiction involves looking for the author's main idea. Sometimes authors explain topics in terms of people having problems and searching for solutions to those problems. Thus, to understand the main idea of this type of nonfiction, the reader needs to be able to determine the real-life problem and the solutions that people have created to solve the problem. Signal words in this type of text include _if, then, effect, resulting in, because, problem, solve, solution, possibilities, think, plans, idea,_ and _determined._

To facilitate the comprehension of problem/solution nonfiction texts, you can show students a blank organizer, like the ones shown in Figure 1.27, before they read. This gives them schema for the type of text structure they will encounter. Thus, they know they'll have to look for the problem in the title or pictures, and then for ways that people attempted to solve it.

Figure 1.27 ■ Sample Graphic Organizers for Problem/Solution Text

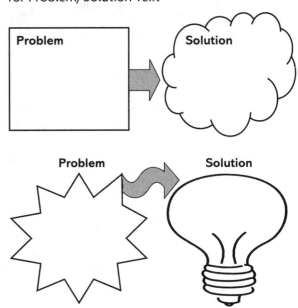

Figure 1.28 ■ Report Frame for Problem/Solution Text

> **Title:** _____
>
> **Author:** _____
>
> The author of this book tells about the problem of _____ .
>
> To solve this problem, _____ did _____ .
>
> Then, _____ .

Additionally, a report frame like the one in Figure 1.28 helps them organize their thoughts for writing about this type of text.

Comprehension Strategies

Good readers are easily recognizable; they can figure out the author's meaning. They do more than simply call out words; they make inferences and predictions, draw conclusions, critically choose information, and create mental pictures while they read. After reading, good readers respond to the text by reflecting, making personal connections, and articulating their ideas about what they've read. There are many strategies that are helpful for showing your students how to do these things, and facilitating their comprehension as a result. This section offers just a few activities, ideas, or lesson plans that you can add to your repertoire of teaching skills to promote comprehension.

■ Critical Reading with Websites

As users of the Internet, your students are bombarded with information they cannot—or should not—use. Thus, it is essential that they develop critical reading skills so that they can make sound decisions about which websites are credible and useful (Alvermann, Moon, & Hagood, 1999; Leu, 2002). Choosing appropriate sources from the web is far different from choosing information from conventional sources such as textbooks and encyclopedias. Careful and selective reading of an array of formats is necessary.

The following is a step-by-step list of teaching suggestions for critical reading of a website. A sample lesson demonstrates how Mr. Yatsko, a sixth grade teacher, followed this plan as he modeled and explained to his students how to choose web-based text for the purpose of writing a report on the presidents.

Choosing a Website for a Report on a President

1. **With the students, brainstorm ways that "surfing the net" is difficult when looking for specific information.**

   Mr. Yatsko said, "Class, each of you has chosen a U.S. President to study, and now it's time to begin looking for information for your report. Today, I'd like you to try to find at least one good website that gives you information on the president you've chosen. As you know, when you're searching the Internet, you'll find a lot of stuff! What have you noticed about searching for information on the Internet?"

Michael spoke up. "Sometimes," he said, "I'll type in a word and it will say, 'This page is not available.' I don't like that."

"Yeah," said Pete. "I hate it when somebody gives me a good website to look up and I can't find it."

Brianna said, "Lots of times I'll find tons of stuff. Once I did a report on Native Americans and I found so much information. I didn't know where to put it all."

"If I get bored, I just click on another page," said Joey.

"Yeah, me too," said Brandon.

"And sometimes," added Mr. Yatsko, "When you search for information, you get websites that are hard to read, or the author of the website just doesn't know what he's talking about! Perhaps you have the problem I have with searching the Internet. My problem is that when I get to a website that I like, there are so many hypertext links that I get distracted because I want to look at them all! So, it's important to know how to stick to your task and to be able to choose the websites that will be most useful to you. Today, we're going to practice doing that while you search for information for your report. Let's go to the computer lab and I'd like for you to sit at a computer with your partner."

2. **At the computer screen, model and explain as you search for information for a specific topic. Show the students how to narrow choices, focus only on the most pertinent information, and ignore links that do not look as if they will be of immediate help. Explain, as you move through the sites, why you have chosen to ignore some links and click on others.**

The students moved to computer tables in the computer lab. Mr. Yatsko said, "Ok, now, we'll use this time to find some information on the U.S. President that you've chosen to research. But first, I want to show you some of the things that I do to make this process a little simpler. I'm going to click on to a website and think out loud for you. Watch the screen while I do this."

Mr. Yatsko accessed the Yahooligans home page, then typed in "U.S. Presidents." He pointed his finger to his forehead and said, "Ok, now, I've got a page from Yahooligans that tells me all the possibilities available for my subject, the presidents. I've chosen to do some research on Harry S. Truman, so I want to find his name on this page somewhere. Ok, look, I've found a list called 'Sites' on this page. And under it, there's a long list of presidents' names. And if I scroll down . . . . Oh, yes! It's a list of all the presidents, alphabetized. Ok, I'll scroll down again . . . Great! I found Harry S. Truman. I'll click on his name, and see what I get. Ok, now, there's a link called 'Categories.' Under 'Categories,' I see 'Harry S. Truman Pictures,' and then I see 'Speeches.' Well, I've decided not to look for pictures yet. And I'm not interested in speeches. All I want to know right now is some basic information about Truman, so I'll need to find a website that contains a brief biography of his life. I don't want too many details yet. Ok, so, down below, I see 'Sites,' and there are eight listed. Each site is named, and there's a little description of it. Just scanning over this list, I am going to pick the one that seems to be the least complicated! Look at number four. It says, 'Harry S. Truman—biography of the 33rd president.' And this is the only website on the list that claims to be a biography. So, I'll click on it. Hmm, first, I'll scroll down the page. Looks good. It's in nice, big print. And it's only one page long. That makes it manageable for me to read right now. And, I don't see any links to other places. That's actually a good thing right now, because I don't want to read speeches, view videos, or otherwise get distracted. I'll read this one, write down some information, and then decide where to look next."

3. **Be sure to emphasize the importance of using a child-friendly search engine such as Yahooligans.**

Mr. Yatsko continued, "Now take a look at the URL, which is the address for this website: http://www.whitehouse.gov/history/presidents/ht33.html.

I can find out the publisher of this website by looking at the URL, before the first single slash mark. It says 'whitehouse.gov.' This is a site about the White House, and its writers must have produced a special webpage on the lives of each of our presidents. I'm rather confident that this site will be reliable. That's not always the case, so that's why I check it out each time I make a search. Another thing I need to do is to be sure this website is safe. Using a kids' search engine like Yahooligans makes me confident that it is ok."

4. **Bookmark links or sites that may be useful later.**

Mr. Yatsko said, "OK, I'll bookmark this page, and print it. There are other sites about Truman that I'd like to look at later. For now, I'll record information from this one in my notes."

5. **Afterwards, ask students to help make a list of the procedures you used. Create a chart.**

Mr. Yatsko said to the students, "As you can see, there are lots of things to think about as you choose a website to read for information. What are some of the things that I looked for or did as I saw the webpage? Talk to your partner about that for a moment. Then, turn your idea into a question and write it down to share with us. For example, one of the things I did was check the website to see if it was easy to read. So, my question would be, 'Is the website easy to read?' Be ready to share the questions that you think of."

6. **From the chart, make a checklist such as the following one that can be used during each search.**

The students talked with each other for a few moments, and then wrote their questions. Several students shared their ideas, while Mr. Yatsko wrote them on chart paper. Later, he incorporated their list into an evaluation checklist, shown in Figure 1.29.

7. **Give students a chance to practice. Ask everyone to begin a search for information they will need to complete a project, report, or assignment.**

The next day, Mr. Yatsko showed the evaluation sheet to his students on the overhead projector. He said, "I've written the questions you thought of yesterday in this checklist. There are ten of them—all important questions to ask. I'd like for you to try to use this list when you do a web search for your report on presidents."

Figure 1.29 ■ Checklist for Evaluating Websites for Research

Name of the website: _____

URL: _____

My purpose for using this website:

Ten Questions to Ask Yourself About the Website

First, be sure that you use a search engine that will find sites that are safe and appropriate for kids, such as Yahooligans. Second, find a website that you think will be useful. Then, answer these questions:

1. Does the website load quickly?
2. Does the website have links that work?
3. Is the website easy to navigate?
4. Does the website have a contact person listed?
5. Is the website written by a knowledgeable and reliable person or group?
6. Why did the author write the website? (To inform? To persuade? To entertain?)
7. Are the words on the website easy to read?
8. Does the website have information that you can use?
9. Is the website fun to use?
10. Does the website have graphics and color that are appealing?

■ Opinion Statements

Everyone's reaction to a single piece of literature is different, depending on their background knowledge, their experiences, their interests, and their development. You can help your students' literacy growth by encouraging their aesthetic responses to books, even if their opinions differ from your own, or from their peers.

To prepare this activity, write several statements about a book that your students have read. These statements should be open-ended in that the reader could either agree or disagree with them. For example, one statement for *The Giver* (Lowry, 1993) would be, "The people in Jonas' community are happier than they would be if they knew the memories." Put each statement on a strip of paper. Students can draw a strip from a box, read it, and then write their reaction in a reading journal. They must state that they agree or disagree, and explain why, showing quotes from the text that support their answers.

Shown in Figure 1.30 is an example of this activity for the story, *Morning Girl* (Dorris, 1992). This story is about the lives of a sister and brother in the West Indies, in the year 1492. The story ends with the arrival of Christopher Columbus.

Figure 1.30

Opinion Statements for *Morning Girl* by Michael Dorris
Christopher Columbus was a good and admirable man.   Agree or Disagree?
Morning Girl was very intelligent.   Agree or Disagree?
Star Boy was ignorant.   Agree or Disagree?
Now Morning Girl's life is going to completely change.   Agree or Disagree?

■ Predicting

One of the strategies that good readers use as they tackle print is that of making predictions. When encouraging predictions, it is important to stick to the topic. Lucy Calkins (2001) warns against asking children to offer too much information before they read, which may lead to distractions and discussions that wander from the topic. According to Williams (1993), this can actually impede comprehension.

Thus, when asking students to make predictions, ask them to justify them. Predictions are not "right," or "wrong;" however, to be acceptable, they should be justified or rationalized. Your students' predictions should make sense, based on the information that has been given to them in the text, in combination with their own ideas based on past experiences. Shown in Figure 1.31 are some charts that you can use to help students record their predictions.

Figure 1.31 ■ Prediction Charts

Prediction Chart with Space for Writing Clues

| **BEFORE READING** |
| This is what I think will happen: |
| This is my clue for making this prediction: |
| **AFTER READING** |
| This is what actually happened: |

Prediction Chart with Reasons and Confirmation

What I Predict Will Happen	Why I Am Making This Prediction	What Actually Happened
Page: _____		
Page: _____		
Page: _____		
Page: _____		

■ Questions for Literature Response

There are many occasions when you need to ask your students questions about litera-ture—guided reading, reading and writing workshop, literature circles, individual reading conferences. The questions shown below focus on the literary elements of fiction, and the structure of text in nonfiction. They can be used as discussion ques-tions, writing prompts, comprehension questions, or extensions for students who need to go beyond the literal text. You can also duplicate them and give them to stu-dents as questions to ask each other during buddy reading or literature circles, or to serve as models when teaching students how to ask questions of each other.

Fiction

Questions about the character
- Why did [*the main character*] act in this manner? What makes you think so?
- What would happen if we put [*the main character*] in another situation, such as _____?
- Are [*the main character's*] actions right? Why or why not?

Questions about the setting
- Suppose this story took place in another place or time, such as _____. What would happen?
- Tell how the setting in this story reminds you of a place or time in real life.

Questions about the events
- Which of these events is the funniest/saddest/scariest? Why?
- Tell what you were thinking when _____ happened.

Questions about the resolution
- How would you have solved the problem differently?
- Why does the author end the story in this manner?
- What lessons were learned by the characters?

Questions about the theme
- Why did the author write this story?
- What lessons can you learn from these characters?
- What is the purpose of this story?
- What other story does this remind you of?

Nonfiction
- What is the author trying to teach you in this selection?
- What is the author's point?
- What have you learned here that you did not know before?
- What is the sequence of events in this book/section/chapter?
- Is something being compared to something else? What is it? How are they alike/different?

- What was the problem? How was it solved?
- Something happened. What was it? What made that happen?
- What new words have you learned? What do they mean?
- What is the most interesting fact in this book? Why?
- What surprised you?
- What did you notice about _____?

■ Visualization

Visual imagery enables readers to understand text, because mental pictures bring the author's words to life in the reader's mind. Some authors are especially skilled at evoking mental images that are familiar to young children; but some expository text does get bogged down in facts, weights, measurements, and figures. Thus, it is important to show students how to make mental pictures of the text. A chart or bookmark with reminders, along with mental modeling, will help. The following is a step-by-step procedure for planning a lesson that encourages visualization skills. A sample social studies lesson demonstrates how one teacher followed this procedure.

Teaching Visualization Skills

1. **Choose a passage from nonfiction text that lends itself to visual imagery. Read the passage aloud.**

   To show his seventh grade students how visual imagery can help them understand this passage from a social studies textbook, Mr. Staples copied it and showed it to his students on the projection screen:

   > Immigrants, such as the Irish, have brought unique contributions to the United States from their homelands all over the world. The United States is sometimes called a "melting pot," a "salad bowl," or a "patchwork quilt" to illustrate how U.S. society combines aspects of many cultures. Some features may blend into the culture of the United States, while others retain their original characteristics. (Bednarz, Miyares, Schug, & White, 2003, p. 87).

2. **Model by thinking out loud, telling of the mental imagery that you create when reading this passage. Tell about the clues that help you make mind pictures, such as descriptive words, specialized vocabulary, or your own experiences. Make a sketch of the image as you talk.**

   Mr. Staples modeled by thinking out loud. He pointed to his forehead and said:
   "As I read this, I get a picture in my head of what the authors are trying to say. The first sentence tells me that immigrants have contributed to our country. I'm not sure what kinds of contributions they are talking about, so I'll read further. The second sentence tells me that several interesting terms are applied to the United States, such as 'melting pot,' 'salad bowl,' or 'patchwork quilt.' These terms tell how our society combines many cultures. Well, I'm not sure what a 'melting pot' is, but I do know what a salad bowl and a quilt look like. Since I eat salads everyday, let me try picturing the 'salad bowl' idea. I like a

salad with lots of different vegetables, in addition to my lettuce. I can even see my salad bowl in my head. I've got a tomato, cucumber slices, olives, mushrooms, a little bit of corn, and some onion. Here, I'll sketch them, even though I'm not much of an artist. See them? Each vegetable contributes to the colors and the flavor of the salad. They don't all blend together. They each have their own taste, but altogether, they make a great salad. So, maybe the authors are telling me that immigrants bring their own kinds of things to our country. Just like I can throw all these ingredients into my salad bowl, our country is like a bowl, made up of many different ideas, types of music, foods, and traditions. This 'salad bowl' idea also reminds me of all the foods we eat in this country. I know that most of the foods we eat originated in other countries, such as tacos, sushi, and spaghetti!"

3. **Ask students to help make a list of clues that help create mental imagery.**

   Mr. Staples continued by explaining, "Visual imagery is especially important when I read for information. When I try reading from difficult textbooks, it helps to use the words as well as the charts, maps, and graphs on the page to create a picture of the topic the author is trying to teach. Let's make a list, to remind us of the things we can look for as we make mental movies of this textbook. I'll put the first item on it: 'descriptive words.' It helps to look for words that show us what the author is talking about, such as 'salad bowl.' We can also look for descriptives like color words, number words, and adjectives. What other clues help us make a mental picture? Let's list them."

   Clues for Helping Us Visualize Nonfiction
   - Descriptive words
   - Comparisons to things we already know
   - Photographs
   - Maps
   - Charts

4. **Read the remainder of the selection, and stop at another point that evokes visualization. Ask students to describe what they see in their mind's eye to each other, and sketch.**

   Mr. Staples said, "Ok, I'd like for you to read the next page of our social studies textbook together, and try some visualizing. Tell your partner about your mind picture. Draw it as you describe what you see. If there are new ideas that we need to add to our chart, let me know and we'll write it down."

Classroom Management Techniques

Cathy Hayden, a third-grade teacher in Pennsylvania, has graciously welcomed hundreds of my students into her classroom over the years. Whenever my students visited, she immediately got them involved in her third-grade learning community. After leaving, my students are required to write a brief report of their observations. They were to tell about Cathy's classroom environment, focusing on the things she did in her classroom, rather than the physical surroundings of the room. Without fail, every semester, I got reports from students who simply couldn't resist telling me about the red calico curtains on her classroom windows! At first, I was exasperated over my students' preoccupation with the pleasantries of her classroom. Gradually, I began to realize how important this was. Cathy's classroom reminded them of home. The students felt at home there—visitors did, too. It was a comfortable place to learn.

Naturally, curtains in the windows will not make your program. But the atmosphere in this classroom says, "I care. This is a place where you can be yourself, just like home." That is an important beginning point, and sets the tone for all that the teacher does.

On the next few pages, I will show you some simple techniques for managing the classroom in such a way that students see the importance of high expectations for literacy learning, while at the same time feeling comfortable in a thriving, welcoming environment.

■ Class Meetings

When a teacher begins the day with a class meeting, many goals are accomplished. First, he or she maintains a sense of community in the classroom. Second, the students' attention is focused in the direction of goals to be accomplished and strategies to be learned. Finally, the teacher conveys the message that reading and writing are important. Listed below are some suggestions for class meetings.

Ways to Hold Class Meetings

1. Begin each day with a song, chant, or poem. Keep it the same daily, to add to a comfortable routine.

2. Talk together about things to accomplish during the day. Ask students to make some choices about how to manage materials or time. For example, ask, "This morning, we need to read our story from *Frog and Toad All Year* (Lobel, 1976) orally. Would you like to read it with partners or use choral reading with the whole group?"

3. Use the time to talk about birthdays. Celebrate students' birthdays with a song, story, or poem. Talk also about famous people born the same day in history. Whenever possible, make connections to literacy, such as things the famous person wrote, favorite books of the famous person, or books written about the famous person. Talk about the birthday child's qualities, too. See if there are any commonalities.

4. Ask your students to bring a favorite book from home. Have them share it by explaining why it is a favorite, and how it fits into the home routine.

5. Ask your students to bring an item from home—other than a book—that shows their reading habits. For example, children can bring a favorite magazine, newspaper, bookmark, or reading lamp.

6. Invite a guest (the principal, guidance counselor, school staff, community members, or parents) to talk with the children during morning minutes. Ask her to share the contents of her briefcase or book bag with the students. Explain how reading is done in her home or office.

7. Write plans for the day. Discuss them in terms of how these plans help your students grow as readers and writers.

8. Read aloud to your students from a book that relates to a theme or topic being explored in your classroom.

9. Write a simple message together, using interactive writing.

10. In a box or gift bag, place an object that relates to the events of the day, the story students will read in the basal, a project that will take place in science or math, or even the weather. Choose someone to unwrap the "gift" and lead a discussion about what it means. Write a brief account of the students' predictions.

■ Managing Procedures

You've heard the saying, "It's the little stuff that gets you down." Nothing was ever truer in the classroom. You can have the world's most exciting lesson planned, but if you haven't figured out how you and your students will accomplish mundane tasks, your lesson can quickly fall apart. Below are a few ways to manage these small tasks and keep your classroom running smoothly.

Five Checkers.   This technique helps you to be selective about which writing assignments will be checked for grammar, spelling, handwriting, or other writing mechanics (Cunningham, Moore, Cunningham, & Moore, 2000). Place four red checkers and one black checker in a bag or bowl. Hold this up high and ask the student to take one checker. If the student chooses a red checker, the assignment was for practice. If she chooses a black checker, the assignment will be graded.

The Red Line.   To encourage a child to make progress as he works, put a red line on his paper before he starts to write (Watson, 1996). Tell the child that you want to see performance beyond the red line by a designated time. This allows you to glance quickly at his paper at anytime to see how much progress he is making and how well he is using his time.

Deadlines.   Establish the amount of time that a task can take. This helps students organize themselves and it also gives most students some motivation to work. Say things like, "You have two minutes to discuss this problem with your teammates," or "Take 37 seconds to write that down."

Class Constitution.   Write an agreement that everyone will live by. This lists the rules that you agree upon for use in the classroom. You can also include things such as "non-negotiable spelling words" or agreements that everyone will follow, such as, "When we write rough drafts, we will be courteous to our readers." Everyone in the class signs at the bottom of the poster.

Transition Cues.   Whenever your students need to move from one activity to another, provide a signal, such as flicking the lights, or ringing a short chime. This eliminates the need for extra teacher talk.

Wall Cues.   On a bulletin board, post titles of books that students have read in the classroom. Then, use these wall cues in guided reading or reading workshop discussions, asking questions like this one: "Pick a title from the wall. Compare this main character to the one in that one." You can also use this technique with words that you post on the word wall, by asking questions such as, "Find a word on the word wall that means almost the same thing as this word."

Hand Signals.   Sometimes, when you ask students questions, they stop short of an answer. Cathy Hayden, a third grade teacher in Pennsylvania, uses a simple hand signal. She gestures with her hands as if stretching a rubber band. From the first day of school, her students learn that this means to "tell more."

■ Four Corners and Bookmarks

This technique allows you to group students based on their interest in a topic of study. Nancy Steider, first-grade teacher in Pennsylvania, adapted Kagan's (1994) strategy for use with her first graders, so that they could choose a topic to study, and write a simple report of their findings.

1. Choose a topic that has four subtopics. Introduce the topic with the students by reading aloud a related tradebook.

2. Create signs that "advertise" each of the subtopics, and display them in the four corners of the room.

3. In each corner, have resource books about the topic available. Make sure that these books reflect a range of abilities, and look for information in each of the books that would vary, so that each person who chooses a book is finding out something unique about the topic.

4. Insert in each book, on a page that contains important information, a bookmark that contains the following:

   • A question about the topic, which can be answered by reading information on the marked page.

   • A request to draw or write something about the topic.

   The bookmark can be a piece of paper folded in half, with the questions printed on one side of the paper.

5. Ask students to choose the topic that they are most interested in learning, and go to that corner.

6. When students get to the corner, they should choose a book, and then follow the directions on the bookmark to write a short report or fact sheet. The student writes a paragraph or a few sentences that answer the first question, and above that, draws a picture and labels it.

7. All students in the class write their own report. After the reports are written, students share their information with the other students in their corner. Once the entire class has gathered together in one spot, all students' papers can be compiled for a class book, and read together as a class.

Allowing students to go to the corners of their favorite topics allows them to choose their interest and learn some research skills. So that the students are somewhat evenly divided, Nancy asks them to write their two favorite choices a day or two before the project. Thus, she forms the groups ahead of time, which provides more structure.

You can use the four corners strategy with older students as well, but you may want them to be more independent as they research information about their topics.

Take a look at the following example that Nancy used with her first graders when teaching a unit on sea animals.

> There were four animals to choose from for study: whales, sharks, starfish, and seahorses. Nancy inserted a bookmark (from Figure 1.32) in one of the books about whales, on a page about baleen whales:

Figure 1.32 ■ Sample Four Corners Bookmark

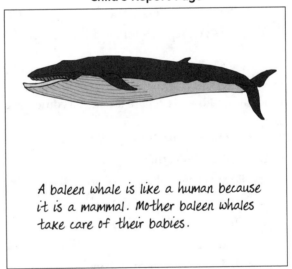

Four Corners Bookmark

Find Out About Baleen Whales

1. On the top of your paper: Draw a picture of a baleen whale. Show the parts of the baleen whale that are different from other whales.

2. On the bottom of your paper, write about this: How is a baleen whale like a human?

Child's Report Page

A baleen whale is like a human because it is a mammal. Mother baleen whales take care of their babies.

■ Independent Reading Management

One of the most important things you can do to develop reading fluency, comprehension, and motivation to read is to provide daily time for independent silent reading. If it is your goal to move beyond standardized testing, and to develop readers who want to read, it makes sense to give your students time to read. Morrow (1991) tells us that children who read voluntarily are the lucky ones in classrooms where teachers give their students opportunities to choose their own books and class time to read them.

You will need a good classroom library, or access to a good school library. Show students, in mini-lessons, how to select books that are at their independent level, using the five-finger rule. To accomplish this, read any page in the book, and count the number of unknown words, starting with the pinky finger. At each unknown word, put one finger down. If, at the end of the page, the thumb is still up, the book is not too hard. Younger readers can use the same idea with three fingers (Allington, 2001).

From the library, students need to select their own books, and have books with them at all times. You can keep a milk crate or durable box near each group of students, so they can house books they will need throughout the day. Another idea is to give students special boxes, bags, or baskets at their desks in which to keep books that are "just right" for them to read independently (Routman, 2003). Establish rules for independent reading time so that your students know what is expected of them and so that they respect this time as an important part of the day (Calkins, 2001; Routman, 2000).

Rules for Independent Reading Time

1. Use the books in your book box or bag.
2. Once you are seated, stay seated.
3. Whisper while reading or read silently.
4. Leave other readers alone unless you are reading with a buddy.
5. Always be prepared for a reading conference with the teacher.

While students are reading independently, use this time for private, quiet reading conferences (Cunningham, Hall, & Defee, 1991, 1998). Inform students in advance about how to prepare for such a conference.

How to Prepare for a Reading Conference with Your Teacher

1. Choose a book that you like and can read.
2. Pick two pages of the book to read aloud to your teacher.
3. Be ready to do one of these things:
   - Tell the teacher why you chose the book.
   - Retell the story.
   - Tell what you learned from the author.
   - Tell the teacher about your predictions and thoughts so far.
   - Tell the teacher what kind of book you are thinking about sharing next week.

■ Guided Reading Management

When you are meeting with a small group for guided reading, the rest of your class needs to be meaningfully engaged. It takes skill, time, and patience for your classroom to run smoothly as you meet with a small group and the remainder of the class works alone. In order for your group to meet successfully, and for the rest of the class to work on things that matter, it is crucial for you to model the kinds of behavior that you expect to see. Nancy Steider, first-grade teacher in Pennsylvania, has told me, "Anytime something goes wrong in my classroom, I realize it's because I didn't model it for them first." Routman (2000) concurs, saying, "Model everything" (p. 162). You will need to show your students things such as what they should do when they need help, how to read alone, how to read with a buddy, and how to handle housekeeping tasks such as sharpening pencils and bathroom use. The following tips will help:

1. Provide water bottles so that trips to the fountain are prevented.
2. Have book boxes or bags near each group of students so no one needs to walk around.
3. Expect students to spend their time reading independently or working on a piece of writing that is related to their reading.
4. Display the assignment or choices of activities.
5. Assign reading partners. Have them choose a permanent spot for reading. They do not need to read the same book together, but must share their books with each other when finished. They must also offer support for each other while reading.
6. Provide taped books at a listening center.
7. At the end of the guided reading group, give students an assignment that is connected to their reading. Have them write it in their reading journals before they leave the group.

But what do you do with the rest of the class while working with one group in a guided reading exercise? The following list offers some suggestions for ways your class can be actively and appropriately engaged while you conduct guided reading groups.

Things for Everyone Else to Do While the Teacher Conducts Guided Reading Groups

1. Read with your reading buddy.
2. Read independently.
3. Find a favorite quotation from the book you just read. Copy it in your reading log and tell what it reminds you of.
4. Write a set of questions for someone else to answer about the book.
5. Keep a log of questions that you want to answer. Write some questions that come to mind as you read your book.
6. Find a quote in the book that gives you a picture in your mind. Write it and then draw that picture.
7. Before you read, make a prediction. Tell why you made it. Find out if your prediction came true. If it didn't, write what actually happened.
8. While reading information, look for the answers to questions your teacher gave you. Use a highlighter to mark the places where you find the answers.
9. Listen to a taped book.
10. Practice a Readers' Theater story script.
11. Summarize the story you read.
12. Summarize the important facts in the chapter or book that you read.

13. List the facts in the article you read.

14. Design a bookmark to go with the book you read.

15. When you find out about something new in your textbook, compare it to something you already know. Draw the comparison.

16. Sketch the plot of your story.

17. Make a map of the setting of your story.

18. Write a letter to the author.

19. Make a list of words that are difficult. Use strategies to figure them out, and then draw pictures to illustrate what they mean.

20. Create a graphic organizer for the book.

Rubrics for Analyzing Writing

"Now I want to give you a homework assignment"—muffled groans—"that I'm sure you'll all enjoy. "—mumblings of unbelief—Tonight on Channel 7 at 8 P.M. there is going to be a special about a famous underwater explorer—Jacques Cousteau. I want everyone to watch. Then write one page telling what you learned."

"A whole page?"

"Yes."

"Does spelling count?"

"Doesn't spelling always count, Gary?"

■ *Bridge to Terabithia* (Paterson, 1977)

When "spelling counts," along with the other features of good writing, it is helpful to have a rubric for assessing these features. Thus, I have included the rubrics shown on the following pages. I created these rubrics using the six traits suggested by Vicki Spandel (2001). "Traits" are all of the characteristics or features of good writing, which, when used cohesively, make the written piece a strong one. Thus, if a piece has all of these traits, its readers would agree that it has quality. The traits Spandel lists in her work are: ideas, organization, voice, word choice, sentence fluency, and conventions. Grade levels one through five are included, as well as a rubric for middle school grades. At each grade level and for each trait, there are separate rubrics for story writing and nonfiction writing, with the exception of conventions. At the end of the section for each grade level, I have listed the rubric for conventions for that grade level, applicable to all types of writing. As Spandel suggests, I used a 5-point scale on the rubrics, with descriptors listed for points of 5, 3, and 1. Scores of 4 and 2 indicate that the writing is at transitional levels. The traits are listed separately on the rubrics so that you can focus on one trait at a time as you read your students' work. You can select the traits you want to assess on any given assignment, or you can assess them all for a comprehensive evaluation. Summary sheets are also included at each grade level.

Because many states have modeled their writing standards on the six-trait system of analyzing writing, it is easy to align standards with these rubrics. For example, Pennsylvania Department of Education standards for writing require students to write with "sharp, distinct focus, identifying topic, task, and audience" (Pennsylvania

Department of Education, 1999, p. 10, available on-line April 11, 2006). Spandel describes one of the traits, "ideas," this way: "The paper is clear, focused, purposeful, and enhanced by significant detail that captures the reader's interest" (2001, p. 49). Similarities like these make it possible to align state standards to the rubrics you will see on the following pages.

Benchmarks will help you determine specific capabilities that you can expect from your students at each level. For example, you'll see the following benchmark for first grade story writing: "The story clearly contains the most basic elements of story: character(s) with a problem that is eventually solved." This benchmark is one for the trait of "organization." If you read a first-grade writer's story, and then decide that it fits this description, he earns a "5," which is the best score possible.

These grade level benchmarks are helpful because sometimes, state standards do not specify grade-by-grade capabilities and must be adapted by teachers and school districts that use them. Some of the benchmarks that I have included here were adapted from the writing benchmarks developed and used by teachers in Pennsylvania (Berks County Intermediate Unit, 2000).

Rubric for Analyzing Student Writing
First Grade—Story Writing

Name of Child: _____

Title or Description of Paper: _____

TRAIT #1: IDEAS (First Grade, Story Writing)

5	3	1
The writer clearly writes a single story line. His or her ideas are all clearly related to this story.	The writer seems to have a story in mind, but strays occasionally from the story line.	The writer does not express thoughts about a single story. The writing contains many disconnected sentences that do not seem to tell a story.
Relevant title and pictures are present.	Title and/or pictures are present but need more clarity.	The title and pictures are absent, or they are present but not relevant at all.

Score for Ideas (Story Writing): _____

TRAIT #2: ORGANIZATION (First Grade, Story Writing)

5	3	1
The story clearly contains the most basic elements of story: character(s) with a problem that is eventually solved.	The story introduces character(s) but the problem and its resolution are not always clear.	The story line is hard to distinguish. Character(s) and problem are not clear.
The sequence of events is clearly evident, with a definitive beginning, middle, and end.	Parts of the beginning, middle, and end are apparent.	There is no clear beginning, middle, and end to the story.

Score for Organization (Story Writing): _____

TRAIT #3: VOICE (First Grade, Story Writing)

5	3	1
The reader knows who is narrating the story without question.	The writer sometimes shifts voice or does not make voice clear from the beginning.	The writer seems indifferent or uninvolved.

Score for Voice (Story Writing): _____

TRAIT #4: WORD CHOICE (First Grade, Story Writing)

5	3	1
The writer always uses nouns and verbs appropriately and effectively.	The writer sometimes uses nouns and verbs appropriately and effectively.	The writer does not use nouns and verbs appropriately or effectively.
The writer uses many descriptive words and phrases.	The writer uses some descriptive words and phrases.	The writer does not attempt to make the writing more interesting. The story is a simple narrative. It appears as if he or she attempts only to use easy-to-spell words.

Score for Word Choice (Story Writing): _____

TRAIT #5: SENTENCE FLUENCY (First Grade, Story Writing)

5	3	1
The story flows well; all sentences connect with each other and are related to the story ideas.	Some sentences connect with each other. Some sentences are choppy or run-on.	Most sentences are unclear, choppy, and disconnected.
The story is pleasant to read and sounds good when read aloud.	The story is fairly pleasant to read and has potential for being smooth and easy to read.	The story does not seem like a story; sentences do not flow together well.

Score for Sentence Fluency (Story Writing): _____

Rubric for Analyzing Student Writing
First Grade—Nonfiction Writing

Name of Child: _____

Title or Description of Paper: _____

TRAIT #1: IDEAS (First Grade, Nonfiction Writing)

5	3	1
The piece shows a strong, clear single topic.	The topic is evident, but the writer occasionally loses focus.	Most details do not connect.
The writer clearly establishes a purpose for the nonfiction piece.	There seems to be a purpose, but the writer does not clearly state it.	The writer's purpose is not evident at all.
Relevant title and pictures are present.	Title and/or some pictures are present but need more clarity.	The title and pictures are absent, or they are present but not relevant at all.

Score for Ideas (Nonfiction Writing): _____

TRAIT #2: ORGANIZATION (First Grade, Nonfiction Writing)

5	3	1
Sentences are related to one main idea.	Some sentences are not related to the main idea.	Most sentences are not related; there does not appear to be a central main idea.
There is definitive sequence to the writing, with a clear beginning, middle, and end.	The beginning, middle, and end are not always clear. Some appropriate parts are missing. It is sometimes hard to follow because the ideas seem to be out of sequence.	There is no sequence to the composition. Sentences are disconnected.

Score for Organization (Nonfiction Writing): _____

TRAIT #3: VOICE (First Grade, Nonfiction Writing)

5	3	1
The reader knows who is narrating the piece without question.	The writer sometimes shifts voice or does not make voice clear from the beginning.	The writer seems indifferent or uninvolved.

Score for Voice (Nonfiction Writing): _____

TRAIT #4: WORD CHOICE (First Grade, Nonfiction Writing)

5	3	1
The writer always uses nouns and verbs appropriately and effectively.	The writer sometimes uses nouns and verbs appropriately and effectively.	The writer does not use nouns and verbs appropriately or effectively.

Score for Word Choice (Nonfiction Writing): _____

TRAIT #5: SENTENCE FLUENCY (First Grade, Nonfiction Writing)

5	3	1
All sentences are appropriate for the topic.	Some sentences connect with each other and the topic. Some sentences are choppy or run on.	Most sentences are unclear, choppy, and disconnected.
The piece is pleasant to read and sounds good when read aloud.	The piece is fairly easy to read and has potential for being smooth and easy to read.	The piece seems more like a list or collection of thoughts; sentences do not flow together well.

Score for Sentence Fluency (Nonfiction Writing): _____

TRAIT #6: CONVENTIONS (First Grade, All Types of Writing)

5	3	1
All common, frequently used words (such as function words) are spelled correctly.	Some common, frequently used words (such as function words) are spelled correctly.	Very few common, frequently used words (such as function words) are spelled correctly, making the piece hard to read.
All invented or sound spellings reveal a pattern of understanding of phonemes.	Some of the invented or sound spellings make sense.	Few, of any, invented or sound spellings reveal a pattern of under-standing of phonemes.
All of the teacher's "non-negotiable words" are spelled correctly.	Some of the teacher's "non-negotiable words" are spelled correctly.	Very few of the "non-negotiable" words are spelled correctly.
Capital letters are always used cor-rectly (first word in sentence, "I," and people's names).	Capital letters are sometimes used correctly (first word in sentence, "I," and people's names).	Capital letters are rarely used cor-rectly (first word in sentence, "I," and people's names).
The following proper end punctuation is always used: • Period • Question mark	The following proper end punctuation is sometimes used: • Period • Question mark	The following proper end punctuation is rarely, if ever, used: • Period • Question mark
All sentences are complete.	Some sentences are complete. Some are fragments or run-on sentences.	Complete sentences are rarely, if ever, used. Most are fragments or run-on sentences.

Score for Conventions (All Types of Writing): _____

Summary Page—First Grade

Name of Child: _____

Title or Description of Paper: _____

Teacher: _____

Type of Writing: _____

Summary of Scores

Ideas: _____

Organization: _____

Voice: _____

Word Choice: _____

Sentence Fluency: _____

Conventions: _____

Overall notes or comments based on analysis of all six traits:

Rubric for Analyzing Student Writing
Second Grade—Story Writing

Name of Child: _____

Title or Description of Paper: _____

TRAIT #1: IDEAS (Second Grade, Story Writing)

5	3	1
The writer clearly writes a single story line. His or her ideas are all clearly related to this story.	The writer seems to have a story in mind, but strays occasionally from the story line.	The writer does not express thoughts about a single story. The writing contains many disconnected sentences that do not seem to tell a story.
The writer offers interesting and unique ideas and creates a strong impression.	Some parts of the story are interesting and unique, leaving the reader wishing for more detail or description. The story shows promise but does not leave a strong impression.	The writing contains mostly disconnected sentences that do not seem to tell a story.
Relevant title and pictures are present. The pictures are well matched to the story. Details in drawings match the details in the story.	Title and/or pictures are present but need more clarity. Some details are present.	The title or pictures are absent, or they are present but not relevant at all.

Score for Ideas (Story Writing): _____

TRAIT #2: ORGANIZATION (Second Grade, Story Writing)

5	3	1
The story clearly contains all of these literary elements: setting, character, problem, events, and resolution. The writer is clearly able to tell a story in its entirety.	The story is easy to follow, but at least one of the elements of story is missing or not well developed.	The story line is hard to distinguish. Most story elements are nonexistent or not clear.
The beginning, middle, and end are clearly evident, with signal words where appropriate.	The beginning, middle, and end are apparent but lacking necessary signal words.	There is no clear beginning, middle, and end to the story. Sequence of events in the story is not logical.

Score for Organization (Story Writing): _____

TRAIT #3: VOICE (Second Grade, Story Writing)

5	3	1
The reader knows who is narrating the story without question.	The writer sometimes shifts voice or does not make voice clear from the beginning.	The writer seems indifferent or uninvolved.
It is clear that the writer kept the audience in mind as he or she wrote the story.	The writer seems to be aware of an audience, but does not always address that audience. Sometimes, it seems as if the writer is only writing for the teacher or for himself or herself.	The writer does not at all appear to be aware of an audience reading the story.

Score for Voice (Story Writing): _____

TRAIT #4: WORD CHOICE (Second Grade, Story Writing)

5	3	1
The writer always uses nouns and verbs appropriately and effectively.	The writer sometimes uses nouns and verbs appropriately and effectively.	The writer does not use nouns and verbs appropriately or effectively.
The writer uses many appropriate descriptive words and phrases that make the story interesting, colorful and lively.	There are some descriptive words and phrases, which give the story potential for being interesting, colorful and lively.	The writer does not attempt to make the story more interesting with descriptions. It appears as if he or she attempts only to use easy-to-spell words.
The writer always uses verbs that show action and make the reader "see" the events in the story.	Some verbs are passive or not descriptive of the action or events in the story.	Action verbs are not used. Passive verbs such as "is," "are," "was," "were," "go," and "went" are consistently used.

Score for Word Choice (Story Writing): _____

TRAIT #5: SENTENCE FLUENCY (Second Grade, Story Writing)

5	3	1
The story flows well; all sentences connect with each other and are related to the story ideas.	Some sentences connect with each other. Some sentences are choppy or run-on.	Most sentences are unclear, choppy, and disconnected.
The story is pleasant to read and sounds good when read aloud.	The story is fairly pleasant to read and has potential for being smooth and easy to read.	The story does not seem like a story; most sentences do not flow together well.
The writer effectively uses statements as well as questions in his/her writing, resulting in smooth and fluent story-telling.	The writer uses some statements and questions, but the effect is not smooth or fluent.	The writer does not vary sentence type at all.

Score for Sentence Fluency (Story Writing): _____

Rubric for Analyzing Student Writing
Second Grade—Nonfiction Writing

Name of Child: _____

Title or Description of Paper: _____

TRAIT #1: IDEAS (Second Grade, Nonfiction Writing)

5	3	1
The piece shows a strong, clear single topic.	The topic is evident, but the writer occasionally loses focus.	Most details do not connect.
The writer clearly establishes a purpose for the nonfiction piece.	There seems to be a purpose, but the writer does not clearly state it.	The writer's purpose is not evident at all.
The piece holds the reader's attention, creates a strong impression about the topic, and offers interesting and unique ideas.	Parts of the piece are interesting and unique, but the reader is left wishing for more detail or description.	The writing contains mostly disconnected sentences that do not seem to explain the topic.

(continued)

5	3	1
Relevant title and pictures are present. The pictures are well matched to the story. Details in drawings match the details in the story.	Title and/or pictures are present but need more clarity. Some details are present.	The title and pictures are absent, or they are present but not relevant at all.

Score for Ideas (Nonfiction Writing): _____

TRAIT #2: ORGANIZATION (Second Grade, Nonfiction Writing)

5	3	1
There is a clear and distinct main idea with related supporting sentences.	The piece is sometimes clear. A main idea is evident, with some sentences supporting it.	A main idea is not evident. Most sentences are disconnected.
There is a definitive sequence to the writing. The writer develops a sequence of events in chronological order, always using signal words (i.e., "first," "next," "then," "finally") where needed.	There is a sequence of events in chronological order, but signal words (i.e., "first," "next," "then," "finally") are not always used where needed.	There is no clear sequence of events or appropriate use of signal words.

Score for Organization (Nonfiction Writing): _____

TRAIT #3: VOICE (Second Grade, Nonfiction Writing)

5	3	1
The reader knows who is narrating the piece without question.	The writer sometimes shifts voice or does not make voice clear from the beginning.	The writer seems indifferent or uninvolved.
It is clear that the writer knows his or her audience and writes for that audience.	The writer seems to have a sense of audience; however, the writing sometimes loses focus on that audience.	There is no sense of audience in the piece.

Score for Voice (Nonfiction Writing): _____

TRAIT #4: WORD CHOICE (Second Grade, Nonfiction Writing)

5	3	1
The writer always uses nouns and verbs appropriately and effectively.	The writer sometimes uses nouns and verbs appropriately and effectively.	The writer does not use nouns and verbs appropriately or effectively.
The writer uses many appropriate descriptive words that make the piece colorful, visible, and lively.	There are some descriptive words and phrases, which give the piece potential for being colorful, visible, and lively.	The writer does not attempt to make the piece more interesting with descriptions. It appears as if he or she attempts only to use easy-to-spell words.
The writer always uses verbs that show action and make the reader "see" the writing.	Some verbs are passive or not descriptive of the action. Terms or ideas are sometimes assumed rather than explained.	Action verbs are not used. Passive verbs such as "is," "are," "was," "were," "go," and "went" are consistently used.

Score for Word Choice (Nonfiction Writing): _____

TRAIT #5: SENTENCE FLUENCY (Second Grade, Nonfiction Writing)

5	3	1
The piece flows well; most sentences connect with each other and are related to the topic.	Some sentences connect with each other. Some sentences are choppy or run-on.	Most sentences are unclear, choppy, and disconnected.
The piece is pleasant to read and sounds good when read aloud.	The piece is fairly pleasant to read and has potential for being smooth and easy to read.	The piece seems more like a list or collection of thoughts; sentences do not flow together well.
The writer effectively uses statements as well as questions in his/her writing, resulting in smooth and fluent reporting.	The writer uses some statements and questions, but the effect is not smooth or fluent.	The writer does not vary sentence type at all.

Score for Sentence Fluency (Nonfiction Writing): _____

TRAIT #6: CONVENTIONS (Second Grade, All Types of Writing)

5	3	1
All common, frequently used words (such as function words) are spelled correctly.	Some common, frequently used words (such as function words) are spelled correctly.	Very few common, frequently used words (such as function words) are spelled correctly, making the piece hard to read.
All invented or sound spellings reveal a pattern of understanding of phonemes.	Some of the invented or sound spellings make sense.	Few, if any, invented or sound spellings reveal a pattern of understanding of phonemes.
All of the teacher's "non-negotiable words" are spelled correctly.	Some of the teacher's "non-negotiable words" are spelled correctly.	Most "non-negotiable" words are spelled incorrectly.
Capital letters are always used correctly (first word in sentence, "I," and names of people and places).	Capital letters are sometimes used correctly (first word in sentence, "I," and names of people and places).	Capital letters are rarely used correctly (first word in sentence, "I," and names of people and places).
The following proper end punctuation is always used: • Period • Question mark • Exclamation mark	The following proper end punctuation is sometimes used: • Period • Question mark • Exclamation mark	The following proper end punctuation is rarely, if ever, used: • Period • Question mark • Exclamation mark
All sentences are complete.	Some sentences are complete. Some sentences are fragments or run-on sentences.	Complete sentences are rarely, if ever, used; fragments and run-on sentences permeate the piece.
All of the following parts of speech are used correctly: • Nouns • Pronouns • Verbs • Adjectives	Some of the following parts of speech are used correctly: • Nouns • Pronouns • Verbs • Adjectives	Few, if any, of the following parts of speech are used correctly: • Nouns • Pronouns • Verbs • Adjectives

Score for Conventions (All Types of Writing): _____

Summary Page—Second Grade

Name of Child: _____

Title or Description of Paper: _____

Teacher: _____

Summary of Scores

Ideas: _____

Organization: _____

Voice: _____

Word Choice: _____

Sentence Fluency: _____

Conventions: _____

_____

Overall Notes or Comments:

Rubric for Analyzing Student Writing
Third Grade—Story Writing

Name of Child: _____

Title or Description of Paper: _____

TRAIT #1: IDEAS (Third Grade, Story Writing)

5	3	1
The writer clearly writes a single story line. His or her ideas are all clearly related to this story.	The writer seems to have a story in mind, but strays occasionally from the story line.	The writer does not express thoughts about a single story. The writing contains many disconnected sentences that do not seem to tell a story.
The writer offers interesting and unique plot twists or events that hold the reader's attention.	Some parts of the story are interesting and unique, yet leaving the reader wishing for more detail, description, or originality.	The story is flat or lifeless.
The writer clearly has an awareness of style throughout the story.	The writer's storytelling is, at times, stylistic but for the most part, the storytelling is rather straightforward.	The writer's style is not apparent. He or she seems to have written this as a simple response to an assignment.
Relevant title and pictures are present. The pictures are well matched to the story. Details in drawings match the details in the story.	Title and/or pictures are present but need more clarity. Some details are present.	The title and pictures are absent, or they are present but not relevant at all.

Score for Ideas (Story Writing): _____

TRAIT #2: ORGANIZATION (Third Grade, Story Writing)

5	3	1
The story clearly contains all of these literary elements: setting, character, problem, events, and resolution. The writer is clearly able to tell a story in its entirety.	The story is easy to follow, but at least one of the elements of story is missing or not well developed.	The story line is hard to distinguish. Most story elements are not clear.
The beginning, middle, and end are clearly evident, with signal words where appropriate.	The beginning, middle, and end are apparent but lacking necessary signal words.	There is no clear beginning, middle, and end to the story.
The sequence of events is plausible and leads to a satisfying resolution.	The story makes sense, but some of the events are not plausible or the resolution does not satisfy the reader.	Most events are not logical, the resolution is nonexistent, or the story ends abruptly.

Score for Organization (Story Writing): _____

TRAIT #3: VOICE (Third Grade, Story Writing)

5	3	1
The reader knows who is narrating the story without question.	The writer sometimes shifts voice or does not make voice clear from the beginning.	The writer seems indifferent or uninvolved.

(continued)

5	3	1
It is clear that the writer kept the audience in mind as he or she wrote the story.	The writer seems to be aware of an audience, but does not always address that audience. Occasionally, it seems as if the writer is only writing for the teacher or for himself or herself.	The writer does not appear to be aware of an audience reading the story.
The tone and flavor of the writing fits the story well.	The story line is clear; however, the tone and flavor of the story are not strong.	There is no tone or flavor to the story; it is a simple narration of events.

Score for Voice (Story Writing): _____

TRAIT #4: WORD CHOICE (Third Grade, Story Writing)

5	3	1
The writer always uses nouns and verbs appropriately and effectively.	The writer sometimes uses nouns and verbs appropriately and effectively.	The writer does not use nouns and verbs appropriately or effectively.
The writer uses many appropriate descriptive words and phrases that make the story interesting, colorful and lively.	There are some descriptive words and phrases, which give the story potential for being interesting, colorful and lively.	The writer does not attempt to make the writing more interesting with descriptions. The story is a simple narrative. It appears as if he or she attempts only to use easy-to-spell words.
The writer always uses verbs that show action and make the reader "see" the events in the story.	Some verbs are passive or not descriptive of the action or events in the story.	Action verbs are not used. Passive verbs such as "is," "are," "was," "were," "go," and "went" are consistently used.
The writer experiments with words to use interesting and unusual terms, and avoids the use of "tired words."	Words used are sufficient to tell the story clearly, but there are some "tired words."	"Tired words" permeate the story.

Score for Word Choice (Story Writing): _____

TRAIT #5: SENTENCE FLUENCY (Third Grade, Story Writing)

5	3	1
The story flows well; all sentences connect with each other and are related to the story ideas. Very few, if any, sentences begin with "and," "then," "but," or "so."	Some sentences connect with each other. Some sentences are choppy or run-on. Some sentences begin with "and," "then," "but," or "so."	Most sentences are unclear, choppy, and disconnected. Most sentences begin with "and," "then," "but," or "so."
The story is pleasant to read and sounds good when read aloud.	The story is fairly pleasant to read and has potential for being smooth and easy to read.	The story does not seem like a story; sentences do not flow together well.
The writer uses a variety of sentence types, such as questions, statements, commands, and exclamations, resulting in smooth and fluent storytelling.	The writer uses some, but not much, variety of sentence types.	The writer does not vary sentence structure or type at all.
The writer uses many sentences of varying lengths.	The writer's sentences are mostly the same length.	The writer's sentences do not vary in length.

Score for Sentence Fluency (Story Writing): _____

Rubric for Analyzing Student Writing
Third Grade—Nonfiction Writing

Name of Child: _____

Title or Description of Paper: _____

TRAIT #1: IDEAS (Third Grade, Nonfiction Writing)

5	3	1
The piece shows a strong, clear single topic.	The topic is evident, but the writer occasionally loses focus.	Most details do not connect.
The writer clearly establishes a purpose for writing this informational piece.	The writer seems to have a purpose for writing the piece; however, the writing occasionally strays from the purpose.	The writer's purpose is not evident at all.
The piece holds the reader's attention, creates a strong impression about the topic, and offers interesting and unique ideas.	Parts of the piece are interesting and unique, but the reader is left wishing for more detail or description.	The writing contains mostly disconnected sentences that do not seem to explain the topic.
The writer clearly has an awareness of style throughout the piece.	The writer's ability to explain facts is sometimes stylistic.	The writer's style is not apparent. He or she seems to have written this as a simple response to an assignment.
Relevant title and pictures are present. The pictures are well matched to the story. Details in drawings match the details in the written piece.	Title and/or pictures are present but need more clarity. Some details are present.	The title and pictures are absent, or they are present but not relevant at all.

Score for Ideas (Nonfiction Writing): _____

TRAIT #2: ORGANIZATION (Third Grade, Nonfiction Writing)

5	3	1
There is a clear and distinct main idea with related supporting sentences.	The piece is sometimes clear. A main idea is evident, with some sentences supporting it.	A main idea is not evident. Most sentences are disconnected.
There is a definitive sequence to the writing. The writer develops a sequence of events in chronological order, always using signal words (i.e., "first," "next," "then," "finally") where needed.	There is a sequence of events in chronological order, but signal words (i.e., "first," "next," "then," "finally") are not always used where needed.	There is no clear sequence of events or appropriate use of signal words.
The writer incorporates interesting and relevant details that pertain to the topic.	Some details are included; some of them stray from the topic.	Many details do not relate to the topic, making the reader wonder about their relevance.

Score for Organization (Nonfiction Writing): _____

TRAIT #3: VOICE (Third Grade, Nonfiction Writing)

5	3	1
The reader knows who is narrating the piece without question.	The writer sometimes shifts voice or does not make voice clear from the beginning.	The writer seems indifferent or uninvolved.
It is clear that the writer knows his or her audience and writes for that audience.	The writer seems to have a sense of audience; however, the writing sometimes loses focus on that audience.	There is no sense of audience in the piece.

Score for Voice (Nonfiction Writing): _____

TRAIT #4: WORD CHOICE (Third Grade, Nonfiction Writing)

5	3	1
The writer always uses nouns and verbs appropriately and effectively.	The writer sometimes uses nouns and verbs appropriately and effectively.	The writer does not use nouns and verbs appropriately or effectively.
The writer uses many appropriate descriptive words that make the piece colorful, visible, and lively.	There are some descriptive words and phrases, which give the piece potential for being colorful, visible, and lively.	The writer does not attempt to make the writing more visible with descriptions. It appears as if he or she attempts only to use easy-to-spell words.
The writer always uses verbs that show action and make the reader "see" the writing.	Some verbs are passive or not descriptive of the action.	Action verbs are not used. Passive verbs such as "is," "are," "was," "were," "go," and "went" are consistently used.
The writer experiments with words to use interesting and unusual terms and avoids the use of "tired words."	Words used are sufficient to report the information, but there are some "tired words."	"Tired words" permeate the piece.
The writer clearly defines all terms and explains all ideas well.	Some of the writer's terms and explanation of ideas are satisfactory.	The writer does not define terms or explain ideas.

Score for Word Choice (Nonfiction Writing): _____

TRAIT #5: SENTENCE FLUENCY (Third Grade, Nonfiction Writing)

5	3	1
The piece flows well; sentences connect with each other and are related to the topic. Very few, if any, sentences begin with "and," "then," "but," or "so."	Some sentences connect with each other. Some sentences are choppy or run-on. Some sentences begin with "and," "then," "but," or "so."	Most sentences are unclear, choppy, and disconnected. Most sentences begin with "and," "then," "but," or "so."
The piece is pleasant to read and sounds good when read aloud.	The piece is fairly pleasant to read and has potential for being smooth and easy to read.	The piece seems more like a list or collection of thoughts; sentences do not flow together well.
The writer uses a variety of sentence types, such as questions, statements, commands, and exclamations, resulting in smooth and fluent reporting.	The writer uses some, but not much, variety of sentence types.	The writer does not vary sentence structure or type at all.
The writer uses many sentences of varying lengths and complexity.	The writer's sentences are mostly the same length. A few sentences are complex; many are simple.	The writer's sentences do not vary in length. Sentences are simple, and many are not complete.

Score for Sentence Fluency (Nonfiction Writing): _____

TRAIT #6: CONVENTIONS (Third Grade, All Types of Writing)

5	3	1
All common, frequently used words (such as function words) are spelled correctly.	Some common, frequently used words (such as function words) are spelled correctly.	Very few common, frequently used words (such as function words) are spelled correctly, making the piece hard to read.
All invented or sound spellings reveal a pattern of understanding of phonemes.	Some of the invented or sound spellings make sense.	Few, of any, invented or sound spellings reveal a pattern of understanding of phonemes.
All of the teacher's "non-negotiable words" are spelled correctly.	Some of the teacher's "non-negotiable words" are spelled correctly.	Most "non-negotiable" words are spelled incorrectly.
Capital letters are always used correctly (first word in sentence, "I," and names of people and places).	Capital letters are sometimes used correctly (first word in sentence, "I," and names of people and places).	Capital letters are rarely used correctly (first word in sentence, "I," and names of people and places).
The following proper end punctuation is always used: • Period • Question mark • Exclamation mark • Comma in series	The following proper end punctuation is sometimes used: • Period • Question mark • Exclamation mark • Comma in series	The following proper end punctuation is rarely, if ever, used: • Period • Question mark • Exclamation mark • Comma in series
All sentences are complete.	Some sentences are complete. Some sentences are fragments or run-on sentences.	Complete sentences are rarely, if ever, used. Fragments and run-on sentences permeate the piece.
All of the following parts of speech are used correctly: • Nouns • Pronouns • Verbs • Adjectives • Conjunctions	Some of the following parts of speech are used correctly: • Nouns • Pronouns • Verbs • Adjectives • Conjunctions	Few, if any, of the following parts of speech are used correctly: • Nouns • Pronouns • Verbs • Adjectives • Conjunctions
The following types of complete sentences are always used correctly: • Simple • Declarative • Interrogative • Exclamatory • Imperative	The following types of complete sentences are sometimes used correctly: • Simple • Declarative • Interrogative • Exclamatory • Imperative	The following types of complete sentences are rarely, if ever, used correctly: • Simple • Declarative • Interrogative • Exclamatory • Imperative

Score for Conventions (All Types of Writing): _____

Summary Page—Third Grade

Name of Child: _____

Title or Description of Paper: _____

Teacher: _____

Summary of Scores

Ideas: _____

Organization: _____

Voice: _____

Word Choice: _____

Sentence Fluency: _____

Conventions: _____

_____

Overall Notes or Comments:

Rubric for Analyzing Student Writing
Fourth Grade—Story Writing

Name of Child: _____

Title or Description of Paper: _____

TRAIT #1: IDEAS (Fourth Grade, Story Writing)

5	3	1
The writer clearly writes a single story line. His or her ideas are all clearly related to this story.	The writer seems to have a story in mind, but strays occasionally from the story line.	The writer does not express thoughts about a single story. The writing contains many disconnected sentences that do not seem to tell a story.
The writer offers interesting and unique plot twists or events that hold the reader's attention.	Some parts of the story are interesting and unique, yet leaving the reader wishing for more detail, description, or originality.	The story is flat or lifeless.
The writer clearly has an awareness of style throughout the story.	The writer's storytelling is, at times, stylistic but for the most part, the storytelling is rather straightforward.	The writer's style is not apparent. He or she seems to have written this as a simple response to an assignment.
The writer experiments with stylistic devices that successfully create a vivid impression and make the story unique.	The writer tells the story well, but does not use stylistic devices successfully.	The story is unclear or rambling. It appears to be not much more than a narrative. No stylistic devices are attempted.
Relevant title is present and piques the reader's curiosity about the story.	Title is present but needs more clarity or interest.	The title is absent, or present but not relevant at all.

Score for Ideas (Story Writing): _____

TRAIT #2: ORGANIZATION (Fourth Grade, Story Writing)

5	3	1
The story clearly contains all of the literary elements: setting, character, problem, events, and resolution. The writer is clearly able to tell a story in its entirety.	The story is easy to follow, but at least one of the elements of story is missing or not well developed.	The story line is hard to distinguish. Most story elements are not clear.
The beginning, middle, and end are clearly evident, with signal words where appropriate.	The beginning, middle, and end are apparent but lacking necessary signal words.	There is no clear beginning, middle, and end to the story.
The sequence of events is plausible and leads to a satisfying resolution.	The story makes sense, but the events are not plausible or the resolution does not satisfy the reader.	Most events are not logical, the resolution is nonexistent, or the story ends abruptly.
The writer always uses meaningful transitions between sentences and paragraphs.	The writer sometimes uses meaningful transitions between sentences and paragraphs.	The writer does not use meaningful transitions between sentences and paragraphs.

Score for Organization (Story Writing): _____

TRAIT #3: VOICE (Fourth Grade, Story Writing)

5	3	1
The reader knows who is narrating the story without question.	The writer sometimes shifts voice or does not make voice clear from the beginning.	The writer seems indifferent or uninvolved.
It is clear that the writer kept the audience in mind as he or she wrote the story.	The writer seems to be aware of an audience, but does not always address that audience. Occasionally, it seems as if the writer is only writing for the teacher or for himself or herself.	The writer does not appear to be aware of an audience reading the story.
The tone and flavor of the writing fits the story well.	The story line is clear; however, the tone and flavor of the story are not strong.	There is no tone or flavor to the story; it is a simple narration of events.
The story is compelling; it grabs the reader's attention because it seems to be written just for him or her.	The story is interesting, but not compelling. The writer seems to be holding back.	The story does not involve or move the reader.

Score for Voice (Story Writing): _____

TRAIT #4: WORD CHOICE (Fourth Grade, Story Writing)

5	3	1
The writer always uses nouns and verbs appropriately and effectively.	The writer sometimes uses nouns and verbs appropriately and effectively.	The writer does not use nouns and verbs appropriately or effectively.
The writer uses many appropriate descriptive words and phrases that make the story interesting, colorful and lively.	There are some descriptive words and phrases, which give the story potential for being interesting, colorful and lively.	The writer does not attempt to make the writing more interesting with descriptions. The story is a simple narrative. It appears as if he or she attempts only to use easy-to-spell words.
The writer always uses verbs that show action and make the reader "see" the events in the story.	Some verbs are passive or not descriptive of the action or events in the story.	Action verbs are not used. Passive verbs such as "is," "are," "was," "were," "go," and "went" are consistently used.
The writer uses interesting and unusual terms, and avoids use of "tired words."	Words used are sufficient to tell the story clearly, but there are some "tired words."	"Tired words" permeate the story.
The writer's words are precise and paint pictures of the story in the reader's mind.	The writer sometimes uses words that are precise, but does not always succeed at painting a vivid picture of the story.	The writer's words are not precise enough to show the reader what he or she means.

Score for Word Choice (Story Writing): _____

TRAIT #5: SENTENCE FLUENCY (Fourth Grade, Story Writing)

5	3	1
The story flows well; all sentences connect with each other and are related to the story ideas. Very few, if any, sentences begin with "and," "then," "but," or "so."	Some sentences connect with each other. Some sentences are choppy or run-on. Some sentences begin with "and," "then," "but," or "so."	Most sentences are unclear, choppy, and disconnected. Most sentences begin with "and," "then," "but," or "so."
Sentences invite natural and expressive oral reading.	The story has potential for being smooth and easy to read; some sentences are rather mechanical and do not invite expression.	The writing does not seem like a story; sentences do not flow together well. The reader must reread to understand the story.

(continued)

5	3	1
The writer uses a variety of sentence types, such as questions, statements, commands, and exclamations, resulting in smooth and fluent storytelling.	The writer uses some, but not much, variety of sentence types.	The writer does not vary sentence structure or type at all.
The writer uses many sentences of varying length and complexity.	The writer's sentences are sometimes the same length. Some sentences are complex; many are simple.	The writer's sentences do not vary in length. Most sentences are simple, and many of them are incomplete.

Score for Sentence Fluency (Story Writing): _____

Rubric for Analyzing Student Writing
Fourth Grade—Nonfiction Writing

Name of Child: _____

Title or Description of Paper: _____

TRAIT #1: IDEAS (Fourth Grade, Nonfiction Writing)

5	3	1
The piece shows a strong, clear single topic.	The topic is evident, but the writer occasionally loses focus.	Most details do not connect.
The writer clearly establishes a purpose for writing this informational piece.	The writer seems to have a purpose for writing the piece; however, the writing occasionally strays from the purpose.	The writer's purpose is not evident at all.
The piece holds the reader's attention, creates a strong impression about the topic, and offers interesting and unique ideas.	Parts of the piece are interesting and unique, but the reader is left wishing for more detail or description.	The writing contains mostly disconnected sentences that do not seem to explain the topic.
The writer clearly has an awareness of style throughout the piece.	The writer's ability to explain facts is sometimes stylistic.	The writer's style is not apparent. He or she seems to have written this as a simple response to an assignment.
Relevant title is present and piques the reader's curiosity about the piece.	Title is present but needs more clarity or interest.	The title is absent, or present but not relevant at all.

Score for Ideas (Nonfiction Writing): _____

TRAIT #2: ORGANIZATION (Fourth Grade, Nonfiction Writing)

5	3	1
There is a clear main idea with related supporting sentences.	The piece is sometimes clear. A main idea is evident, with some sentences supporting it.	A main idea is not evident. Most sentences are disconnected.
The writer organizes information and explains it using a logical structure: description, sequence, compare/contrast, cause/effect, or problem/solution.	The writer explains the topic well but does not organize it or structure it in one of the text structures.	The writer does not explain the topic or organize information in a logical fashion.
The writer incorporates interesting and relevant details that pertain to the topic.	Some details are included; some of them stray from the topic.	Many details do not relate to the topic, making the reader wonder about their relevance.

(continued)

5	3	1
The writer always uses meaningful transitions between sentences and paragraphs.	The writer sometimes uses meaningful transitions between sentences and paragraphs.	The writer does not use meaningful transitions between sentences and paragraphs.

Score for Organization (Nonfiction Writing): _____

TRAIT #3: VOICE (Fourth Grade, Nonfiction Writing)

5	3	1
The reader knows who is narrating the piece without question.	The writer sometimes shifts voice or does not make voice clear from the beginning.	The writer seems indifferent or uninvolved.
It is clear that the writer knows his or her audience and writes for that audience.	The writer seems to have a sense of audience; however, the writing occasionally loses focus on that audience.	There is no sense of audience in the piece.

Score for Voice (Nonfiction Writing): _____

TRAIT #4: WORD CHOICE (Fourth Grade, Nonfiction Writing)

5	3	1
The writer always uses nouns and verbs appropriately and effectively.	The writer sometimes uses nouns and verbs appropriately and effectively.	The writer does not use nouns and verbs appropriately or effectively.
The writer uses many appropriate descriptive words and phrases that make the piece colorful, visible, and lively.	There are some descriptive words and phrases, which give the piece potential for being colorful, visible, and lively.	The writer does not attempt to make the writing more interesting with descriptions. It appears as if he or she attempts only to use easy-to-spell words.
The writer always uses verbs that show action and make the reader "see" the events in the piece.	Some verbs are passive or not descriptive of the action.	Action verbs are not used. Passive verbs such as "is," "are," "was," "were," "go," and "went" are consistently used.
The writer consistently uses interesting and unusual terms, and avoids use of "tired words."	Words used are sufficient to report the information clearly, but there are some "tired words."	"Tired words" permeate the piece.
The writer clearly defines all terms and explains all ideas well.	Some of the writer's terms and explanation of ideas are satisfactory.	The writer does not define terms or explain ideas.
The writer's words are precise and paint pictures of the topic in the reader's mind.	The writer sometimes uses words that are precise, but does not always succeed at painting a vivid picture of the topic.	The writer's words are not precise enough to show the reader what he or she means.

Score for Word Choice (Nonfiction Writing): _____

TRAIT #5: SENTENCE FLUENCY (Fourth Grade, Nonfiction Writing)

5	3	1
The piece flows well; sentences connect with each other and are related to the topic. Very few, if any, sentences begin with "and," "then," "but," or "so."	Some sentences connect with each other. Some sentences are choppy or run-on. Some sentences begin with "and," "then," "but," or "so."	Most sentences are unclear, choppy, and disconnected. Most sentences begin with "and," "then," "but," or "so."
Sentences invite natural and expressive oral reading.	The piece has potential for being smooth and easy to read. Some sentences are rather mechanical and do not invite expression.	The piece seems more like a list or collection of thoughts; most sentences do not flow together well. The reader must reread to understand the main idea of the piece.

(continued)

5	3	1
The writer uses a variety of sentence types, such as questions, statements, commands, and exclamations, resulting in smooth and fluent reporting.	The writer uses some, but not much, variety of sentence types.	The writer does not vary sentence structure or type at all.
The writer uses many sentences of varying lengths and complexity.	The writer's sentences are mostly the same length. Some sentences are complex; many are simple.	The writer's sentences do not vary in length. Sentences are simple, and many are not complete.

Score for Sentence Fluency (Nonfiction Writing): _____

TRAIT #6: CONVENTIONS (Fourth Grade, All Types of Writing)

5	3	1
All common, frequently used words (such as function words) are spelled correctly.	Some common, frequently used words (such as function words) are spelled correctly.	Very few common, frequently used words (such as function words) are spelled correctly, making the written piece hard to read.
All of the teacher's "non-negotiable words" are spelled correctly.	Some of the teacher's "non-negotiable words" are spelled correctly.	Most "non-negotiable" words are spelled incorrectly.
Capital letters are always used correctly.	Capital letters are sometimes used correctly.	Capital letters are rarely used correctly.
The following proper end punctuation is always used: • Period • Question mark • Exclamation mark • Comma • Apostrophe	The following proper end punctuation is sometimes used: • Period • Question mark • Exclamation mark • Comma • Apostrophe	The following proper end punctuation is rarely, if ever, used: • Period • Question mark • Exclamation mark • Comma • Apostrophe
All sentences are complete.	Some sentences are complete. Some sentences are fragments or run-on sentences.	Fragments or run-on sentences permeate the piece.
All of the following parts of speech are used correctly: • Nouns • Pronouns • Verbs • Adjectives • Conjunctions • Adverbs	Some of the following parts of speech are used correctly: • Nouns • Pronouns • Verbs • Adjectives • Conjunctions • Adverbs	Few, if any, of the following parts of speech are used correctly: • Nouns • Pronouns • Verbs • Adjectives • Conjunctions • Adverbs
The following types of complete sentences are always used correctly: • Simple • Compound • Declarative • Interrogative • Exclamatory • Imperative	The following types of complete sentences are sometimes used correctly: • Simple • Compound • Declarative • Interrogative • Exclamatory • Imperative	The following types of complete sentences are rarely, if ever, used correctly: • Simple • Compound • Declarative • Interrogative • Exclamatory • Imperative

Score for Conventions (All Types of Writing): _____

Summary Page—Fourth Grade

Name of Child: _____

Title or Description of Paper: _____

Teacher: _____

Summary of Scores

Ideas: _____

Organization: _____

Voice: _____

Word Choice: _____

Sentence Fluency: _____

Conventions: _____

Overall Notes or Comments:

Rubric for Analyzing Student Writing
Fifth Grade—Story Writing

Name of Child: _____

Title or Description of Paper: _____

TRAIT #1: IDEAS (Fifth Grade, Story Writing)

5	3	1
The writer clearly writes a single story line. His or her ideas are all clearly related to this story.	The writer seems to have a story in mind, but strays occasionally from the story line.	The writer does not express thoughts about a single story. The writing contains many disconnected sentences that do not seem to tell a story.
The writer offers interesting and unique plot twists or events that hold the reader's attention.	Some parts of the story are interesting and unique, yet leaving the reader wishing for more detail, description, or originality.	The story is flat or lifeless.
The writer clearly establishes his/her own writing style, which remains consistent throughout the story.	The writer's storytelling is, at times, stylistic but is, for the most part, rather straightforward.	The writer's style is not apparent. He or she seems to have written this as a simple response to an assignment.
The writer uses stylistic devices that successfully create a vivid impression and make the story unique.	The writer tells the story well, but does not use stylistic devices successfully.	The story is unclear or rambling. It appears to be not much more than a narrative. No stylistic devices are attempted.
The story shows originality, creativity, and thought.	The ideas in the story are clear, and there is some evidence of creativity or originality.	Ideas are either not original or not clear.
Relevant title is present and piques the reader's curiosity about the story.	Title is present but needs more clarity or interest.	The title is absent, or present but not relevant at all.

Score for Ideas (Story Writing): _____

TRAIT #2: ORGANIZATION (Fifth Grade, Story Writing)

5	3	1
The story clearly contains all of these literary elements: setting, character, problem, events, and resolution. The writer is clearly able to tell a story in its entirety.	The story is easy to follow, but at least one of the elements of story is missing or not well developed.	The story line is hard to distinguish. Most story elements are not clear.
The beginning, middle, and end are clearly evident, with signal words where appropriate.	The beginning, middle, and end are apparent but lacking necessary signal words.	There is no clear beginning, middle, and end to the story.
The sequence of events is plausible and leads to a satisfying resolution.	The story makes sense, but the events are not plausible or the resolution does not satisfy the reader.	Most events are not logical, the resolution is nonexistent, or the story ends abruptly.
The writer always uses meaningful transitions between sentences and paragraphs.	The writer sometimes uses meaningful transitions between sentences and paragraphs.	The writer does not use meaningful transitions between sentences and paragraphs.

Score for Organization (Story Writing): _____

TRAIT #3: VOICE (Fifth Grade, Story Writing)

5	3	1
The reader knows who is narrating the story without question.	The writer sometimes shifts voice or does not make voice clear from the beginning.	The writer seems indifferent or uninvolved.
It is clear that the writer kept the a udience in mind as he or she wrote the story.	The writer seems to be aware of an audience, but does not always address that audience. Occasionally, it seems as if the writer is only writing for the teacher or for himself or herself.	The writer does not appear to be aware of an audience reading the story.
The tone and flavor of the writing fit the story well.	The story line is clear; however, the tone and flavor of the story are not strong.	There is no tone or flavor to the story; it is a simple narration of events.
The story is compelling; it grabs the reader's attention because it seems to be written just for him or her.	The story is interesting, but not compelling. The writer seems to be holding back.	The story does not involve or move the reader.

Score for Voice (Story Writing): _____

TRAIT #4: WORD CHOICE (Fifth Grade, Story Writing)

5	3	1
The writer always uses nouns, verbs, adjectives, and adverbs effectively to convey meaning.	The writer sometimes uses nouns, verbs, adjectives, and adverbs effectively to convey meaning.	The writer uses nouns, verbs, adjectives, and adverbs ineffectively.
The writer uses many appropriate descriptive words and phrases that make the story interesting, colorful, and lively.	There are some descriptive words and phrases, which give the story potential for being interesting, colorful, and lively.	The writer does not attempt to make the writing more interesting with descriptions. It appears as if he or she attempts only to use easy-to-spell words.
The writer always uses verbs that show action and make the reader "see" the events in the piece.	Some verbs are passive or not descriptive of the action .	Action verbs are not used. Passive verbs such as "is," "are," "was," "were," "go," and "went" are consistently used.
The writer uses interesting and unusual terms and avoids use of "tired words."	Words used are sufficient to tell the story clearly, but there are some "tired words."	"Tired words" permeate the story.
The writer's words are precise and paint pictures of the story in the reader's mind.	The writer sometimes uses words that are precise, but does not always succeed at painting a vivid picture of the story.	The writer's words are not precise enough to show the reader what he or she means.

Score for Word Choice (Story Writing): _____

TRAIT #5: SENTENCE FLUENCY (Fifth Grade, Story Writing)

5	3	1
The story flows well; all sentences connect with each other and are related to the story ideas. Very few, if any, sentences begin with "and," "then," "but," or "so."	Most sentences connect with each other. Some sentences are choppy or run-on. Some sentences begin with "and," "then," "but," or "so."	Sentences are unclear, choppy, and disconnected. Most sentences begin with "and," "then," "but," or "so."
Sentences invite natural and expressive oral reading.	The story has potential for being smooth and easy to read; some sentences are rather mechanical and do not invite expression.	The writing does not seem like a story; sentences do not flow together well. The reader must reread to understand the story.
The writer uses a variety of sentence types, such as questions, statements, commands, and exclamations, resulting in smooth and fluent storytelling.	The writer uses some, but not much, variety of sentence types.	The writer does not vary sentence structure or type at all.
The writer uses many sentences of varying length and complexity.	The writer's sentences are mostly the same length. Some sentences are complex; many are simple.	The writer's sentences do not vary in length. Most sentences are simple, and many of them are incomplete.
The writer writes realistic and effective dialogue between characters.	The writer attempts dialogue but some of it is unrealistic or ineffective.	The writer does not attempt to write dialogue at all.

Score for Sentence Fluency (Story Writing): _____

Rubric for Analyzing Student Writing
Fifth Grade—Nonfiction Writing

Name of Child: _____

Title or Description of Paper: _____

TRAIT #1: IDEAS (Fifth Grade, Nonfiction Writing)

5	3	1
The piece shows a strong, clear single topic.	The topic is evident, but the writer occasionally loses focus.	Most details do not connect.
It is clear that there is a specific purpose for the paper; the writer uses only relevant statements and facts for this purpose and audience.	The purpose for the paper competes with some irrelevant statements or facts.	There is no evident purpose for this piece, or, the piece is too short to determine the purpose.
The piece holds the reader's attention, creates a strong impression about the topic, and offers interesting and unique ideas.	Parts of the piece are interesting and unique, but the reader is left wishing for more detail or description.	The writing contains mostly disconnected sentences that do not seem to explain the topic.
The writer clearly has an awareness of style throughout the piece.	The writer's ability to explain facts is sometimes stylistic.	The writer's style is not apparent. He or she seems to have written this as a simple response to an assignment.

(continued)

5	3	1
The writer presents the information in an original, creative, and thoughtful manner.	The ideas in the piece are clear, and there is some evidence of creativity or originality.	Ideas are either not original or not clear.
Relevant title is present and piques the reader's curiosity about the piece.	Title is present but needs more clarity or interest.	The title is absent, or present but not relevant at all.

Score for Ideas (Nonfiction Writing): _____

TRAIT #2: ORGANIZATION (Fifth Grade, Nonfiction Writing)

5	3	1
There is a clear main idea with related supporting sentences.	The piece is sometimes clear. A main idea is evident, with some sentences supporting it.	A main idea is not evident. Most sentences are disconnected.
The writer organizes information and explains it using a logical structure: description, sequence, compare/contrast, cause/effect, or problem/solution.	The writer explains the topic well but does not organize it or structure it in one of the five text patterns.	The writer does not explain the topic or organize information in a logical fashion.
The writer uses appropriate signal words that signify text structure.	Text structure is evident but signal words are either not used or used inappropriately.	The writer does not attempt to use text structure or signal words.
The writer incorporates interesting and relevant details that pertain to the topic.	Some details are included; some of them stray from the topic.	Many details do not relate to the topic, making the reader wonder about their relevance.
The writer always uses meaningful transitions between sentences and paragraphs.	The writer sometimes uses meaningful transitions between sentences and paragraphs.	The writer does not use meaningful transitions between sentences and paragraphs.

Score for Organization (Nonfiction Writing): _____

TRAIT #3: VOICE (Fifth Grade, Nonfiction Writing)

5	3	1
The reader knows who is narrating the piece without question.	The writer sometimes shifts voice or does not make voice clear from the beginning.	The writer seems indifferent or uninvolved.
It is clear that the writer knows his or her audience and writes for that audience.	The writer seems to have a sense of audience; however, the writing occasionally loses focus on that audience.	There is no sense of audience in the piece.
The piece is compelling; it grabs the reader's attention because it is lively and engages the reader's thoughts. The writer cares about the topic enough to make it interesting.	The piece can be interesting at times, but not compelling. The writer seems to be holding back.	The piece does not involve or move the reader at all. The writer does not seem to care about the topic enough to make it interesting.
It is clear that the writer is knowledgeable about this topic, and offers only relevant facts and details.	While the writer seems knowledgeable about this topic, he/she sometimes offers irrelevant or erroneous information.	The writer does not seem to be knowledgeable about this topic.

Score for Voice (Nonfiction Writing): _____

TRAIT #4: WORD CHOICE (Fifth Grade, Nonfiction Writing)

5	3	1
The writer always uses nouns, adjectives, and adverbs effectively to convey meaning.	The writer sometimes uses nouns, verbs, adjectives, and adverbs effectively to convey meaning.	The writer uses nouns, verbs, adjectives, and adverbs ineffectively.
The writer uses many appropriate descriptive words and phrases, including sense words that make the piece colorful, visible, and lively.	The writer uses a few descriptive words and phrases, which give the piece potential for being colorful, visible, and lively.	The writer does not attempt to make the writing more visible with descriptions. It appears as if he or she attempts only to use easy-to-spell words.
The writer always uses verbs that show action and make the reader "see" the events in the piece.	Some verbs are passive or not descriptive of the action.	Action verbs are not used. Passive verbs such as "is," "are," "was," "were," "go," and "went" are consistently used.
The writer uses interesting and unusual terms, and avoids use of "tired words."	Words used are sufficient to report the information clearly, but there are some "tired words."	"Tired words" permeate the piece.
The writer clearly defines all terms and explains all ideas well.	Some of the writer's terms and explanation of ideas are satisfactory.	The writer does not define terms or explain ideas.
The writer's words are precise and paint pictures of the topic in the reader's mind.	The writer sometimes uses words that are precise, but does not always succeed at painting a vivid picture of the topic.	The writers' words are not precise enough to show the reader what he or she means.

Score for Word Choice (Nonfiction Writing): _____

TRAIT #5: SENTENCE FLUENCY (Fifth Grade, Nonfiction Writing)

5	3	1
The piece flows well; sentences connect with each other and are related to the topic. Very few, if any, sentences begin with "and," "then," "but," or "so."	Some sentences connect with each other. Some sentences are choppy or run-on. Some sentences begin with "and," "then," "but," or "so."	Most sentences are unclear, choppy, and disconnected. Most sentences begin with "and," "then," "but," or "so."
Sentences invite natural and expressive oral reading.	The piece has potential for being smooth and easy to read. Some sentences are rather mechanical and do not invite expression.	The piece seems more like a list or collection of thoughts; most sentences do not flow together well. The reader must reread to understand the main idea of the piece..
The writer uses a variety of sentence types, such as questions, statements, commands, and exclamations, resulting in smooth and fluent reporting.	The writer uses some, but not much, variety of sentence types.	The writer does not vary sentence structure or type at all.
The writer uses many sentences of varying lengths and complexity.	The writer's sentences are mostly the same length. Some sentences are complex; many are simple.	The writer's sentences do not vary in length. Sentences are simple, and many are not complete.

Score for Sentence Fluency (Nonfiction Writing): _____

TRAIT #6: CONVENTIONS (Fifth Grade, All Types of Writing)

5	3	1
All common, frequently used words (such as function words) are spelled correctly.	Some common, frequently used words (such as function words) are spelled correctly.	Very few common, frequently used words (such as function words) are spelled correctly, making the written piece hard to read.
All of the teacher's "non-negotiable words" are spelled correctly.	Some of the teacher's "non-negotiable words" are spelled correctly.	Most "non-negotiable" words are spelled incorrectly.
Capital letters are always used correctly.	Capital letters are sometimes used correctly.	Capital letters are rarely used correctly.
The following proper end punctuation is always used: • Period • Question mark • Exclamation mark • Comma • Apostrophe • Quotation marks	The following proper end punctuation is sometimes used: • Period • Question mark • Exclamation mark • Comma • Apostrophe • Quotation marks	The following proper end punctuation is rarely, if ever, used: • Period • Question mark • Exclamation mark • Comma • Apostrophe • Quotation marks
All sentences are complete.	Some sentences are complete. Some sentences are fragments or run-on sentences.	Fragments or run-on sentences permeate the piece.
All of the following parts of speech are used correctly: • Nouns • Pronouns • Verbs • Adjectives • Conjunctions • Adverbs • Interjections	Some of the following parts of speech are used correctly: • Nouns • Pronouns • Verbs • Adjectives • Conjunctions • Adverbs • Interjections	Few, if any, of the following parts of speech are used correctly: • Nouns • Pronouns • Verbs • Adjectives • Conjunctions • Adverbs • Interjections
The following types of complete sentences are always used correctly: • Simple • Compound • Declarative • Interrogative • Exclamatory • Imperative	The following types of complete sentences are sometimes used correctly: • Simple • Compound • Declarative • Interrogative • Exclamatory • Imperative	The following types of complete sentences are rarely, if ever, used correctly: • Simple • Compound • Declarative • Interrogative • Exclamatory • Imperative

Score for Conventions (All Types of Writing): _____

Summary Page—Fifth Grade

Name of Child: _____

Title or Description of Paper: _____

Teacher: _____

Summary of Scores

Ideas: _____

Organization: _____

Voice: _____

Word Choice: _____

Sentence Fluency: _____

Conventions: _____

Overall Notes or Comments:

Rubric for Analyzing Student Writing
Middle School—Story Writing

Name of Child: _____

Title or Description of Paper: _____

TRAIT #1: IDEAS (Middle School, Story Writing)

5	3	1
The writer clearly writes a single story line. His or her ideas are all clearly related to this story.	The writer seems to have a story in mind, but strays occasionally from the story line.	The writer does not express thoughts about a single story. The writing contains many disconnected sentences that do not seem to tell a story.
The writer offers interesting and unique plot twists or events that hold the reader's attention.	Some parts of the story are interesting and unique, yet leaving the reader wishing for more detail, description, or originality.	The story is flat or lifeless.
The writer clearly establishes his/her own writing style, which remains consistent throughout the story.	The writer's storytelling is, at times, stylistic but is, for the most part, rather straightforward.	The writer's style is not apparent. He or she seems to have written this as a simple response to an assignment.
The writer uses stylistic devices that successfully create a vivid impression and make the story unique.	The writer tells the story well, but does not use stylistic devices successfully.	The story is unclear or rambling. It appears to be not much more than a narrative. No stylistic devices are attempted.
The story shows originality, creativity, and thought.	The ideas in the story are clear, and there is some evidence of creativity or originality.	Ideas are either not original or not clear.
Relevant title is present and piques the reader's curiosity about the story.	Title is present but needs more clarity or interest.	The title is absent, or present but not relevant at all.
The story has a clear theme; the writer makes it clear that he/she had a compelling reason for writing the story.	It is apparent that the writer intended to convey theme; it is not always clear in the story.	Theme is not evident in the story.

Score for Ideas (Story Writing): _____

TRAIT #2: ORGANIZATION (Middle School, Story Writing)

5	3	1
The story clearly contains all of these literary elements: setting, character, problem, events, resolution, and theme. The writer is clearly able to tell a story in its entirety.	The story is easy to follow, but at least one of the elements of story is missing or not well developed.	The story line is hard to distinguish. Most story elements are not clear.
The sequence of events is plausible, and leads to a satisfying resolution.	The story makes sense, but the events are not plausible or the resolution does not satisfy the reader.	Most events are not logical, the resolution is nonexistent, or the story ends abruptly.
The writer always uses meaningful transitions between sentences and paragraphs.	The writer sometimes uses meaningful transitions between sentences and paragraphs.	The writer does not use meaningful transitions between sentences and paragraphs.

(continued)

5	3	1
The story flows smoothly from beginning to end. There are no unanswered questions about events or character traits.	The story has potential for being well-told. There are some unanswered questions about events or character traits.	The story jumps from one event or description to the next without apparent reason. There are many unanswered questions about events or character traits.

Score for Organization (Story Writing): _____

TRAIT #3: VOICE (Middle School, Story Writing)

5	3	1
The reader knows who is narrating the story without question.	The writer sometimes shifts voice or does not make voice clear from the beginning.	The writer seems indifferent or uninvolved.
It is clear that the writer kept the audience in mind as he or she wrote the story.	The writer seems to be aware of an audience, but does not always address that audience. Occasionally, it seems as if the writer is only writing for the teacher or for him or herself.	The writer does not appear to be aware of an audience reading the story.
The tone and flavor of the writing fits the story well.	The story line is clear; however, the tone and flavor of the story are not strong.	There is no tone or flavor to the story; it is a simple narration of events.
The story is compelling; it grabs the reader's attention because it seems to be written just for him/her.	The story is interesting, but not compelling. The writer seems to be holding back.	The story does not involve or move the reader.
The writer establishes a clear and identifiable point of view.	The writer seems to be aware of point of view, but occasionally slips out of this perspective.	There is no clear and identifiable point of view in the story.

Score for Voice (Story Writing): _____

TRAIT #4: WORD CHOICE (Middle School, Story Writing)

5	3	1
The writer always uses nouns, verbs, adjectives, and adverbs effectively to convey meaning.	The writer sometimes uses nouns, verbs, adjectives, and adverbs effectively to convey meaning.	The writer uses nouns, verbs, adjectives, and adverbs ineffectively.
The writer uses many appropriate descriptive words that make the story interesting, colorful, and lively.	There are some descriptive words and phrases, which give the story potential for being interesting, colorful, and lively.	The writer does not attempt to make the writing more interesting with descriptions. It appears as if he or she attempts only to use easy-to-spell words.
The writer always uses verbs that show action and make the reader "see" the events in the story.	Some verbs are passive or not descriptive of the action or events in the story.	Action verbs are not used. Passive verbs such as "is," "are," "was," "were," "go," and "went" are consistently used.
The writer uses interesting and unusual terms and avoids use of "tired words."	Words used are sufficient to tell the story clearly, but there are some "tired words."	"Tired words" permeate the story.

(continued)

5	3	1
The writer uses words that are precise and paint pictures of the story in the reader's mind.	The writer sometimes uses words that are precise, but does not always succeed at painting a vivid picture of the story.	The writer's words are not precise enough to show the reader what he or she means.
The writer's word choices consistently and effectively convey mood that is appropriate for this story.	The writer's word choices sometimes convey mood that is appropriate for the story.	There is no sense of mood appropriate for this story.

Score for Word Choice (Story Writing): _____

TRAIT #5: SENTENCE FLUENCY (Middle School, Story Writing)

5	3	1
The story flows well; sentences connect with each other and are related to the story ideas. Very few, if any, sentences begin with "and," "then," "but," or "so."	Most sentences connect with each other. Some sentences are choppy or run-on. Some sentences begin with "and," "then," "but," or "so."	Sentences are unclear, choppy, and disconnected. Most sentences begin with "and," "then," "but," or "so."
Sentences invite natural and expressive oral reading.	The story has potential for being smooth and easy to read; some sentences are rather mechanical and do not invite expression.	The writing does not seem like a story; sentences do not flow together well. The reader must reread to understand the story.
The writer uses a variety of sentence types, such as questions, statements, and commands, resulting in smooth and fluent storytelling.	The writer uses some, but not much, variety of sentence types.	The writer does not vary sentence structure or type at all.
The writer uses many sentences that are simple as well as compound.	The writer's sentences are sometimes the same length. Some sentences are complex; many are simple.	The writer's sentences do not vary in length or complexity. Most sentences are simple, and many of them are incomplete.
The writer writes realistic and effective dialogue between characters.	The writer attempts dialogue but some of it is unrealistic or ineffective.	The writer does not attempt to write dialogue at all.

Score for Sentence Fluency (Story Writing): _____

Rubric for Analyzing Student Writing
Middle School—Nonfiction Writing

Name of Child: _____

Title or Description of Paper: _____

TRAIT #1: IDEAS (Middle School, Nonfiction Writing)

5	3	1
The piece shows a strong, clear single topic.	The topic is evident, but the writer occasionally loses focus.	Most details do not connect.
It is clear that there is a specific purpose for the paper; the writer uses only relevant statements and facts.	The purpose for the paper competes with some irrelevant statements or facts.	There is no evident purpose for this piece; or, the paper is too short to determine the purpose.
The piece holds the reader's attention, creates a strong impression about the topic, and offers interesting and unique ideas.	Parts of the piece are interesting and unique, but the reader is left wishing for more detail or description.	The writing contains mostly disconnected sentences that do not seem to explain the topic.
The writer uses stylistic devices that successfully create a vivid impression and make the informational piece unique.	The writer explains the topic well, and sometimes uses stylistic devices successfully.	The piece is unclear or rambling. It appears to be not much more than a narrative, with no stylistic devices.
The writer presents the information in an original, creative, and thoughtful manner.	The ideas in the piece are clear, and there is some evidence of creativity or originality.	Ideas are either not original or not clear.
The writer carefully presents facts and always offers reliable sources to back up the information presented.	The writer presents facts and sometimes offers reliable sources to back up the information presented. He or she sometimes offers irrelevant or erroneous information.	The writer is not careful to present facts; opinions and unsubstantiated information permeate the piece. The writer offers much irrelevant or erroneous information.
Relevant title is present and piques the reader's curiosity about the story.	Title is present but needs more clarity or interest.	The title is absent, or present but not relevant at all.

Score for Ideas (Nonfiction Writing): _____

TRAIT #2: ORGANIZATION (Middle School, Nonfiction Writing)

5	3	1
The writer establishes the topic and purpose in the introduction.	A main idea is evident, although it is not established clearly in the introduction.	A main idea is not evident. Sentences are disconnected.
The writer organizes information and explains it using a logical structure: description, sequence, compare/contrast, cause/effect, or problem/solution.	The writer explains the topic well but does not organize it or structure it in one of the five text patterns.	The writer does not explain the topic or organize information in a logical fashion.
The writer uses appropriate signal words that signify text structure.	Text structure is evident but signal words are either not used or used inappropriately.	The writer does not attempt to use text structure or signal words.

(continued)

5	3	1
The writer writes fully developed paragraphs with only the most relevant details that support the stated topic.	The writer sometimes strays from the topic with irrelevant details.	Many details do not relate to the topic, making the reader wonder about their relevance.
The writer always uses meaningful transitions between sentences and paragraphs.	The writer sometimes uses meaningful transitions between sentences and paragraphs.	The writer does not use meaningful transitions between sentences and paragraphs.
The writer closes by restating the topic and purpose in the conclusion.	The writer closes but the topic and purpose are not clearly included in a conclusion.	There is no identifiable conclusion.

Score for Organization (Nonfiction Writing): _____

TRAIT #3: VOICE (Middle School, Nonfiction Writing)

5	3	1
The writer or narrator speaks directly to the reader, personalizing the piece or connecting with the audience.	The writer sometimes shifts voice or does not make voice clear from the beginning.	The writer seems indifferent or uninvolved.
The writer clearly identifies the topic, task, and audience for the paper.	The writer seems to have a topic, task, and audience in mind; however, these are not always clear.	The writer does not seem to have a topic, task, or audience in mind.
The writer establishes a single and clear point of view.	The writer seems to have a point of view in mind; however, it is not always clear.	The writer does not have a point of view.
The writer uses the most effective format or structure for the intended audience and purpose.	The format or structure is somewhat effective but occasionally loses its appeal or focus.	The format or structure is nonexistent or ineffective.
The piece is compelling; it grabs the reader's attention because it is lively and engages the reader's thoughts. The writer cares about the topic enough to make it interesting.	The piece is interesting at times, but not compelling. The writer seems to be holding back.	The piece does not involve or move the reader at all. The writer does not seem to care about the topic enough to make it interesting.
It is clear that the writer is knowledgeable about this topic, and offers only relevant facts and details.	While the writer seems knowledgeable about this topic, he/she sometimes offers irrelevant or erroneous information.	The writer does not seem to be knowledgeable about this topic.

Score for Voice (Nonfiction Writing): _____

TRAIT #4: WORD CHOICE (Middle School, Nonfiction Writing)

5	3	1
The writer always uses nouns, verbs, adjectives, and adverbs effectively to convey meaning.	The writer sometimes uses nouns, verbs, adjectives, and adverbs effectively to convey meaning.	The writer uses nouns, verbs, adjectives, and adverbs ineffectively.
The writer uses many appropriate descriptive words that make the piece colorful, visible, and lively.	There are some descriptive words and phrases, which give the piece potential for being colorful, visible, and lively.	The writer does not attempt to make the writing more interesting with descriptions. It appears as if he or she attempts only to use easy-to-spell words.

(continued)

5	3	1
The writer always uses verbs that show action and make the reader "see" the events in the piece.	Some verbs are passive or not descriptive of the action or events in the piece.	Action verbs are not used. Passive verbs such as "is," "are," "was," "were," "go," and "went" are consistently used.
The writer uses interesting and unusual terms and avoids use of "tired words."	Words used are sufficient to report the information clearly, but there are some "tired words."	"Tired words" permeate the piece.
The writer clearly defines all terms and explains all ideas well.	Some of the writer's terms and explanation of ideas are satisfactory.	The writer does not define terms or explain ideas.
The writer's words are precise and paint pictures of the topic in the reader's mind.	The writer sometimes uses words that are precise, but does not always succeed at painting a vivid picture of the topic.	The writer's words are not precise enough to show the reader what he or she means.
The writer consistently uses words that convey a natural and honest approach to the piece, adding to the overall effectiveness of the piece.	The writer occasionally uses words that seem to be "trying too hard;" the reader sometimes gets the feeling that the writer is merely trying to use "big words."	The writer seems to be uncomfortable with his or her own words, and the piece sounds stilted or unnatural.

Score for Word Choice (Nonfiction Writing): _____

TRAIT #5: SENTENCE FLUENCY (Middle School, Nonfiction Writing)

5	3	1
The piece flows well; all sentences connect with each other and are related to the topic. Very few, if any, sentences begin with "and," "then," "but," or "so."	Some sentences connect with each other. Some sentences are choppy or run-on. Some sentences begin with "and," "then," "but," or "so."	Most sentences are unclear, choppy, and disconnected. Most sentences begin with "and," "then," "but," or "so."
Sentences invite natural and expressive oral reading.	The piece has potential for being smooth and easy to read. Some sentences are rather mechanical and do not invite expression.	The piece seems more like a list or collection of thoughts; most sentences do not flow together well. The reader must reread to understand the main idea of the paper.
The writer uses a variety of sentence types, such as questions, statements, commands, and exclamations, resulting in smooth and fluent reporting.	The writer uses some, but not much, variety of sentence types.	The writer does not vary sentence structure or type at all.
The writer sustains a logical and smooth transition between paragraphs.	The writer uses paragraphs but does not always provide smooth transitions.	The writer's paragraphs do not flow. There are no transitions.
The writer uses many sentences of varying lengths and complexity.	The writer's sentences are sometimes the same length. Some sentences are complex; many are simple.	The writer's sentences do not vary in length. Sentences are simple, and many are not complete.

Score for Sentence Fluency (Nonfiction Writing): _____

TRAIT #6: CONVENTIONS (Middle School, All Types of Writing)

5	3	1
All words are spelled correctly.	Some words are spelled correctly.	Very few words are spelled correctly, making the written piece hard to read.
Capital letters are always used correctly.	Capital letters are sometimes used correctly.	Capital letters are rarely used correctly.
The following proper end punctuation is always used: • Period • Question mark • Exclamation mark • Comma • Apostrophe • Quotation marks • Colon • Semi-colon • Parentheses	The following proper end punctuation is sometimes used: • Period • Question mark • Exclamation mark • Comma • Apostrophe • Quotation marks • Colon • Semi-colon • Parentheses	The following proper end punctuation is rarely used: • Period • Question mark • Exclamation mark • Comma • Apostrophe • Quotation marks • Colon • Semi-colon • Parentheses
All sentences are complete.	Some sentences are complete. Some sentences are fragments or run-on sentences.	Fragments or run-on sentences permeate the piece.
All of the following parts of speech are used correctly: • Nouns • Pronouns • Verbs • Adjectives • Conjunctions • Adverbs • Interjections	Some of the following parts of speech are used correctly: • Nouns • Pronouns • Verbs • Adjectives • Conjunctions • Adverbs • Interjections	Few, if any, of the following parts of speech are used correctly: • Nouns • Pronouns • Verbs • Adjectives • Conjunctions • Adverbs • Interjections
The following types of complete sentences are always used correctly: • Simple • Compound • Declarative • Interrogative • Exclamatory • Imperative	The following types of complete sentences are sometimes used correctly: • Simple • Compound • Declarative • Interrogative • Exclamatory • Imperative	The following types of complete sentences are rarely, if ever, used correctly: • Simple • Compound • Declarative • Interrogative • Exclamatory • Imperative

Score for Conventions (All Types of Writing): _____

Summary Page—Middle School

Name of Child: _____

Title or Description of Paper: _____

Teacher: _____

Summary of Scores

Ideas: _____

Organization: _____

Voice: _____

Word Choice: _____

Sentence Fluency: _____

Conventions: _____

_____

Overall Notes or Comments:

Reading Assessments for the Classroom Teacher

The next day, Mr. Ratburn announced a spelling test for Friday.
"I want you to study very hard," he said. "The test will have a hundred words."
Buster looked pale.

■ *Arthur's Teacher Trouble* (Brown, 1986)

Classroom life is full of tests. But they don't all have to be like Mr. Ratburn's 100-word spelling test. Getting a true picture of your students' reading abilities can be done efficiently, yet without the dread felt by the characters in Marc Brown's book, *Arthur's Teacher Trouble.*

In this section, you will find several assessments that are useful for the classroom teacher who wishes to find out what happens when she or he asks students to read. The reading analyses included are modifications of the running record (Clay, 1985, 2000, 2005), the miscue analysis (Goodman & Goodman, 2004), an oral reading fluency check (Opitz & Rasinski, 1998), and the retelling analysis (Glazer, 1998). My purpose was to make each assessment brief, easy to use, and informative for the teacher with multiple demands on her time and large groups of students. "Mini-Assessments" are brief assessments based on a sample of a child's reading and are taken from the assessment tools listed above. Each Mini-Assessment can be completed separately, or you can complete them all for a more thorough assessment of a child's reading.

The best way to find out how well a student reads is to ask him or her to read and pay close attention to what the child does while reading. Thus, all of these assessments require the student to privately read aloud to you from a short selection. Once you complete a running record of the child's oral reading of a passage, you can assess word recognition, comfort level with the text, use of miscues, rate of reading, fluency, self-monitoring abilities, and retelling abilities.

All of the Mini-Assessments are based on oral reading of about 150-250 words in a text that is usually selected by the teacher, but you can do this assessment by asking the student to select the text. When assessing a child for the first time, choose text that is at his or her approximate grade level. If you know the child, choose text that is at the appropriate instructional level, so that it presents a small challenge to the child without causing frustration. As you listen to the student read, make notations that record his or her reading behaviors. Use the guide shown in Figure 3.1.

Figure 3.1 ■ Notations to Use When Recording Students' Reading Behaviors

Notations for the Running Record
(Adapted from Clay, 2000, 2005)

Children's book text taken from Wiseman (1959)
As the student reads, mark your copy of the text with the notations shown below.

Description of Student's Text Processing Behavior	Notation for Marking on the Copy of the Story
Correct word—This means that the spoken word is the same as the printed word.	Either mark each correct word with a checkmark, or leave the word blank. (If the student is anxious or nervous about making mistakes, mark each correct word with a checkmark.) ✓ ✓ ✓ ✓ ✓ ✓ ✓ ✓ **One day Morris the Moose saw a cow.**
Incorrect or substituted word—The spoken word is not the same as the printed word. These are included in a count of inaccurate words.	Record the student's miscue above the printed word. ✓ ✓ ✓ ✓ mouse ✓ ✓ ✓ **One day Morris the Moose saw a cow.**
Attempts to decode—This is when the student tries to sound out letters or stretch out a word to figure it out. These are noted but not scored.	Record each attempt above the printed word. m-m-moose ✓ ✓ ✓ ✓ ✓ ✓ **One day Morris the Moose saw a cow.**
Self-corrections—If the reader goes back to a miscue and corrects it so that the spoken word is the same as the written word, this is a self-correction. These are not considered inaccurate words.	Record the miscue, and write **SC** above it. SC ✓ ✓ ✓ ✓ mouse ✓ ✓ ✓ **One day Morris the Moose saw a cow.**
Omission—This is when the reader skips over a word or punctuation, leaving it out of the reading. In this modified running record, omissions are noted but not scored.	Record an empty circle above the text word or punctuation mark. ✓ ✓ ✓ ○ ✓ ✓ ✓ ✓ **One day Morris the Moose saw a cow.**
Insertion—This is when the reader adds a word that is not in the text. In this modified running record, insertions are noted but not scored.	Record any inserted word by writing it above a caret, at the place of insertion. ✓ ✓ ✓ ✓ ✓ ✓ ✓ big ✓ **One day Morris the Moose saw a ^ cow.**
Teacher assistance—This is when the reader is "stuck" and stops reading. Wait at least 3–4 seconds before saying, "Try the strategies you know to help you figure it out." If the reader asks for help, make this suggestion: "You try it. Use the strategies that you know." If the student is still unsuccessful, then tell him the word. Count teacher assisted miscues as inaccurate words.	Record **TA** if assistance is needed, and indicate the corrected word, if there is one. ✓ ✓ ✓ ✓ TA ✓ ✓ ✓ **One day Morris the Moose saw a cow.**
Repetition—This is when the reader repeats words, phrases, or sentences. Do not count repetitions as inaccurate words; however, make note of them because they interrupt fluency.	Write ←R above the entire line of text repeated. ✓ ✓ ✓ ✓ ✓ ←——— R **One day Morris the Moose saw a cow.**

Once you have gathered a sample of the child's oral reading, you can find out as much information as you want from one session. Each separate assessment is a "Mini-Assessment." Periodically, you will want to evaluate each child's reading using all of the assessments. On a weekly basis, however, you can simply use one of the Mini-Assessments, depending on the needs of the child and your curriculum. The Mini-Assessments are listed below, along with the essential question that you can answer with each assessment, and each is described on the following pages.

Classroom Reading Mini-Assessments

- Word Recognition Rate—How many words does the student recognize?
- Reader-Text Match—What is the student's reading level?
- Fluency Analysis: Words per Minute—What is the student's reading rate?
- Fluency Analysis: Repetition Frequency—How often does the student repeat words or phrases?
- Self-Regulation—How often does the student correct himself when he makes a miscue?
- Miscue Analysis: Semantically Similar Miscues—How many of the student's miscues make sense in the context?
- Miscue Analysis: Visually Similar Miscues—How many of the student's miscues are graphophonologically similar to the print?
- Retelling Analysis—How well does the student retell the story (fiction) or the important ideas (nonfiction)?

■ Word Recognition Rate

Miscues are utterances and behaviors that differ from what is printed on the page. Thus, if a child makes a miscue, he or she is not translating the text exactly as the author intended. Sometimes, miscues indicate comprehension, even though the spoken word does not match the printed word. For example, a young boy who sees the word *father*, yet says the word *dad*, is telling us that he comprehends the text, even though he doesn't say exactly what he sees on the printed page. Nevertheless, a miscue indicates a less than accurate rendition of the printed text, and most of them are counted in a tally of words read correctly by the student.

Such a tally is called the **Word Recognition Rate**. This rate indicates the percentage of words that the student read exactly as they appear on the page. The following steps explain how to compute this rate.

1. Be sure that you know the exact number of words in the entire passage that the student reads.
2. Count the types of miscues listed below. These are considered inaccurate, regardless of the meaning that they carry. Write their number on the chart shown in Figure 3.2, and add them to determine the total number of inaccurate words.
   - Incorrect or substituted words
   - Teacher-assisted words

Figure 3.2 ■ Word Recognition Rate Mini-Assessment

Student: _____   Student's Grade Level: _____

Date: _____   Title of Selection: _____

Level or approximate readability of selection: _____   # of words: _____

Inaccurate Words	Tally or Number
Incorrect or substituted word	
Teacher assistance	

# of words in text − # of inaccurate words = _____ (# of words read correctly)

Formula for Word Recognition Rate:

$$\frac{\textit{\# of words read correctly}}{\textit{\# of words in the text}}$$

Word Recognition Rate: _____

Anecdotal notes:

3. Next, determine the number of words that the child read correctly. To do that, subtract the total number of inaccurate words from the total number of words in the passage that the child read.

4. Determine the Word Recognition Rate. This is the percentage of words read correctly in the passage. To compute this, divide the number of words read correctly by the number of words in the passage. (See the formula in Figure 3.2.)

5. The result is the Word Recognition Rate, a percentage that indicates how well the student instantly recognizes words on the page.

■ Reader-Text Match

One important determination you will need to make is the reading level of the student, or your best guess at the level of reading materials that your student can handle comfortably. In this Mini-Assessment, the **Reader-Text Match**, you can gather information that will help you decide which books would be appropriate for your students to read independently as well as in instructional situations. The next few steps show you how.

First, determine the Word Recognition Accuracy Rate. (The formula is shown in Figure 3.3; detailed directions are the same as those provided in the previous section.) Next, look at the Text Difficulty table, also shown on the Mini-Assessment form. This table shows the percentages that correspond to independent, instructional, and frustrational levels of text difficulty.

What does this mean? If you know the level or approximate readability of the text that you selected, then you now have a measure of the student's comfort with this level of text. For example, suppose the selection read by your student was approximated at the second grade level, and her Word Recognition Accuracy Rate was 93%. According to the chart in Figure 3.3, your student can read second grade material with some instructional support. Most likely, she would be reading second grade texts in guided reading lessons in the classroom. If this student is in second grade, this means that she is reading on grade level. If she is not in second grade, she is reading either above or below grade level. Remember that this information is gleaned from one passage and one "mini" assessment; therefore, it is important to assess continually throughout the school year. Also keep in mind that results of this assessment might vary, depending on the type of text you use. Be sure to assess with nonfiction texts as well as fiction selections throughout the school year.

Figure 3.3 ■ Reader-Text Match Mini-Assessment

Student: _____   Student's Grade Level: _____

Date: _____   Title of Selection: _____

Level or approximate readability of selection: _____   # of words: _____

Formula for Word Recognition Rate:	**Reading Ability Levels**
$$\frac{\text{\# of words read correctly}}{\text{\# of words in the text}}$$	95%–100%: Independent 90%–94%: Instructional Below 90%: Frustrational

This student read _____% of the words correctly. Using this level of text, the student's

reading level is: _____ .

(independent, instructional, frustrational)

Anecdotal notes:

■ Fluency Analysis: Words Per Minute

The National Reading Panel (2000) states that fluency includes "speed, accuracy, and proper expression" (p. 11). While speed or rate is just one part of fluency, it adds to the total picture of the child as a reader who is comfortable with the text. The steps below show you how to determine a reader's "words per minute" rate.

1. Determine the number of words in a piece of text and ask the child to read it aloud.
2. As he reads, use a stopwatch to time his reading.
3. Determine the **Words Per Minute** (WPM) rate by inserting the number of seconds that it took the child to read into the formula shown on the Mini-Assessment sheet in Figure 3.4.

Figure 3.4 ■ Fluency Analysis: Words per Minute Mini-Assessment

Student: _____   Student's Grade Level: _____

Date: _____   Title of Selection: _____

Level or approximate readability of selection: _____   # of words: _____

Formula for WPM:

$$\frac{\text{\# of words in the text} \times 60}{\text{\# of seconds it took to read the text}}$$

Words Per Minute Rate Norms

First grade	54–79
Second grade	75–100
Third grade	100–124
Fourth grade	115–140
Fifth grade	125–150
Sixth grade	135–170

This student read _____ words per minute, and is/is not within the recommended range for his/her grade level.

Anecdotal notes:

Find the child's grade level on the Reading Rate chart and the corresponding recommended reading rates for each grade level. Check to see if the child's WPM is within the recommended range for his or her grade level. Words per minute rates in this chart are taken from Forman and Sanders (cited in Johns & Bergland, 2002) and from Fountas and Pinnell (2001).

■ Fluency Analysis: Repetition Frequency

Another measure of fluency is an assessment of the student's **repetitions**. Many times, good readers make repetitions because they are anxious, nervous, or unfamiliar with the print. But repetitions can also indicate a discomfort with the text, or with reading aloud. Fluid, smooth reading is desirable, and can be achieved with repeated readings and practice.

To determine a student's repetition frequency, count the number of repetitions he or she makes, and then divide that number into the number of words in the text. This yields a score that indicates approximately how often the reader repeats words or phrases. See the Mini-Assessment in Figure 3.5.

Figure 3.5 ■ Fluency Analysis: Repetition Frequency Mini-Assessment

Student: _____   Student's Grade Level: _____

Date: _____   Title of Selection: _____

Level or approximate readability of selection: _____   # of words: _____

> **Formula for Repetition Frequency:**
>
> $$\frac{\text{\# of words in the text}}{\text{\# of repetitions}} = \underline{\hspace{1cm}} \text{ (Repetition rate)}$$

This student made a repetition approximately every _____th word.

Anecdotal Notes:

■ Self-Regulation

A good reader knows when he or she does not understand a piece of text. **Self-regulation** is a child's ability to question his or her own comprehension, stop and think about it, and use a variety of strategies to correct the misunderstanding. When you examine the record of your students' reading, you will be able to draw many conclusions about how well they regulate their own reading, or their metacognitive abilities. In this Mini-Assessment, count the number of self-corrections made by the reader, as this is indicative of the thought processes manifested by metacognition. The following steps show you how to make these assessments.

1. Find the self-corrections.
2. Find the number of potential inaccurate word miscues. To do this, count the number of incorrect, substituted, or teacher-assisted words. Add this to the number of self-corrections that the student made. This number reveals how many *potential* word recognition errors that student could have made, had he spoken all of these incorrect or substituted words without correcting them. This is called "potential" because if the child had not gone back to self-correct when she or he caught the miscue, you would be counting those miscues as inaccurate word recognition errors.
3. Find the self-correction rate by using the formula shown in Figure 3.6. A high percentage (above 95%) indicates that the reader is regulating his or her reading well enough to correct word errors while reading.

Figure 3.6 ■ Self-Regulation Mini-Assessment

Student: _____ Student's Grade Level: _____

Date: _____ Title of Selection: _____

Level or approximate readability of selection: _____   # of words: _____

Formula for Self-Correction Rate:

$$\frac{\text{\# self-corrections}}{\text{\# of potential inaccurate word miscues}}$$

Potential incorrect word miscues = (# of inaccurate, substituted, or TA words) + (# of self-corrections)

This student self-corrected _____% of his/her potential inaccurate word miscues.

Anecdotal Notes:

■ Semantically Similar Miscues

Paying attention to the miscues that your reader makes will give you a window to her ability to process print. Sometimes readers see a word but say a different, yet semantically similar, word. For example, a reader who says "supper" when he or she sees "dinner" is making a semantically similar miscue. This is important, because it tells you that the student understands this portion of the text, even though he or she did not say the word intended by the author. While semantically similar miscues do not match the print, they do indicate at least some comprehension, because the student is able to produce a word that makes some sense in that context.

Examine each incorrect or substituted word miscue. Ask yourself, "Does this miscue make sense in the context of this selection?" If it does, the child has derived semantic clues from the text, perhaps based on his prior experiences and confirmation of predictions. Record the number of semantically similar miscues on the Mini-Assessment form, shown in Figure 3.7, and determine the percentage of semantic miscues using the formula.

Figure 3.7 ■ Semantically Similar Miscues Mini-Assessment

Student: _____ Student's Grade Level: _____

Date: _____ Title of Selection: _____

Level or approximate readability of selection: _____ # of words: _____

Out of _____ incorrect or substituted word miscues, _____% were semantically similar to the print.

Formula for Percentage of Semantic Miscues:

$$\frac{\text{\# of semantic miscues}}{\text{\# of incorrect or substituted words}}$$

The spoken miscues that made sense within the context are shown below.

Written Text:	Incorrect or Substituted Word That is Semantically Similar:

■ Visually Similar Miscues

Often, the reader says something that is visually similar to the written text. Grapho-phonological clues such as the first letter, or the suffix on the end of the word, may lead a reader to say a word that carries the same phonological traits. For example, a reader might see the word *something* and say the word *sometimes*, or may see the word *music* and say *mice*.

Look again at each miscue. Ask yourself, "Is the miscue similar, graphically or phonologically (or both), to the word in the text?" If it is, the child is using letter/sound cues. The resulting miscue might make sense in the context, but it also might not. Record the percentage of visually similar miscues, using the formula shown in Figure 3.8.

Figure 3.8 ■ Visually Similar Miscues Mini-Assessment

Student: _____ Student's Grade Level: _____

Date: _____ Title of Selection: _____

Level or approximate readability of selection: _____ # of words: _____

Out of _____ incorrect or substituted word miscues, _____% were visually similar to the print.

> **Formula for Percentage of Visual Miscues:**
>
> $$\frac{\text{\# of visually similar miscues}}{\text{\# of incorrect or substituted words}}$$

The spoken miscues that share graphic and/or phonological qualities with the words printed in text are shown below.

Written Text:	Incorrect or Substituted Word That is Visually Similar:

■ Retelling Analysis

After the student reads, ask him or her to retell the selection, telling everything he or she remembers about it. You might say something like this: "Pretend I've never heard this selection before. Tell it to me so that I know what the author wrote." As the child retells, make brief notes about the main points he or she makes or the story elements that are mentioned. When the child is finished, ask questions to prompt him or her to tell more, if necessary. Be sure to indicate in your notes the point at which you needed to use prompts.

Figure 3.9 ■ Retelling of Fiction Mini-Assessment

Story Retelling Analysis

Student: _____   Student's Grade Level: _____

Date: _____   Title of Selection: _____

Level or approximate readability of selection: _____   # of words: _____

Independent	Instructional	Frustrational
The retelling . . .	The retelling . . .	The retelling was . . .
• was full and detailed. • was mostly unassisted. • was correct. • included personal connections or reflections.	• was partial, but satisfactory. • needed to be prompted for about half of the details. • was accurate after questioning or prompting. • was not independently done; some guidance from the teacher required.	• fragmented. • confusing. • incomplete; important details were missing. • indicative of misunderstanding or difficulty with the selection.

Characters			
	Independent	Instructional	Frustrational

Setting (Time and Place)			
	Independent	Instructional	Frustrational

Problem			
	Independent	Instructional	Frustrational

Events			
	Independent	Instructional	Frustrational

Overall retelling rating:			
	Independent	Instructional	Frustrational

Anecdotal notes:

Figure 3.10 ■ Retelling of Nonfiction Mini-Assessment

Nonfiction Text Retelling Analysis

Student: _____   Student's Grade Level: _____

Date: _____   Title of Selection: _____

Level or approximate readability of selection: _____   # of words: _____

Independent	**Instructional**	**Frustrational**
The retelling . . . • was full and detailed. • was mostly unassisted. • was correct. • included personal connections or reflections.	The retelling . . . • was partial, but satisfactory. • needed to be prompted for about half of the details. • was accurate after questioning or prompting. • was not independently done; some guidance from the teacher required.	The retelling was . . . • fragmented. • confusing. • incomplete; important details were missing. • indicative of misunderstanding or difficulty with the selection.

Summarizes the main idea			
Independent	Instructional	Frustrational	N/A

Understands and uses new vocabulary			
Independent	Instructional	Frustrational	N/A

Interprets visual information			
Independent	Instructional	Frustrational	N/A

Describes the subject			
Independent	Instructional	Frustrational	N/A

Makes comparisons			
Independent	Instructional	Frustrational	N/A

Explains cause/effect or problem/solution			
Independent	Instructional	Frustrational	N/A

Tells sequence of events or steps in procedure			
Independent	Instructional	Frustrational	N/A

Makes personal connections to prior knowledge			
Independent	Instructional	Frustrational	N/A

Overall retelling rating:		
Independent	Instructional	Frustrational

Anecdotal notes:

When analyzing the retelling, review your notes. Overall, how well did the child retell the selection? If the selection is fiction, were all story elements included? If it is nonfiction, did the child tell the main idea and include all the important details? Pay attention to the criteria listed on the appropriate retelling analysis sheet, then rate the child's retelling ability on one of the Mini-Assessment Forms shown in Figures 3.9 and 3.10.

Classroom Reading Assessments: The Complete Analysis

To obtain a more complete picture of your students' reading behaviors, you can administer the running record, and assess all of the behaviors listed earlier. While this full assessment requires more of your time, it gives you an analysis of each student's reading from all perspectives: reader-text match, word recognition, reading fluency, self-regulation abilities, use of available clues on the page, and retelling analysis. The form shown in Figure 3.11 (at the end of this section) allows for recording of all of the assessments in the running record.

Looking at all of the information gathered from your student, you get a much broader picture of his or her reading ability. The complete running record allows you to determine an overall reading ability, based on all of these assessments. Sometimes, a student's results on separate assessments seem to conflict. For example, look at the following scenario:

Patrick, a second grader, read a passage from a selection estimated to be at the second grade level. His scores were:

- Word recognition: 93%
- Reader-Text match: Instructional
- Retelling: Frustrational

Looking at the Overall Results Table on the last page of the Running Record Assessments form, you can see that Patrick's overall reading ability with this passage was Frustrational. Thus, while his word recognition score indicated the instructional level, he was unable to retell the story elements sufficiently to assure the teacher that he comprehended what he read. Additionally, other results add some clues to this picture:

- Self-corrections: 50%
- Repetitions: Every eighth word
- Visually similar miscues: 97% of miscues were visually similar
- Semantically similar miscues: 3% of miscues were semantically similar
- Words per minute: 63 WPM (below second grade level)

Patrick's reading is slower than the usual for second grade, with many repetitions. The miscues that he made were dependent upon visual cues, and usually did not make sense. Half of his miscues were corrected. All of this indicates that he is reading this passage slowly, hesitantly, and without comprehension, even though he recognized 93% of the words on the page. Thus, Patrick's teacher would be wise to give him easier materials to read, and use strategies to improve his fluency. Additionally, she can help him capitalize on his self-regulation abilities, pointing out to him how his self-corrections are helpful and can improve his understanding.

You may want to use this complete assessment three or four times a year. Weekly, decide which reading behaviors you need to assess for each child, and use one of the mini-assessments with each child. In a class of about 25 students, you can accomplish this by observing and reading with just four or five students per day. This will help you maintain an on-going assessment of how well your students are reading.

Figure 3.11 ■ The Complete Set of Classroom Reading Assessments

Classroom Reading Assessments: The Complete Analysis

Student: _____ Student's Grade Level: _____

Date: _____ Title of Selection: _____

Level or approximate readability of selection: _____ # of words: _____

1. Word Recognition Rate and Reader-Text Match: What is the student's reading level based on word accuracy?

Tally of Miscues:

Incorrect or Substituted Words—

Teacher Assisted Words—

Formula for Word Recognition Rate:

$$\frac{\text{\# of words read correctly}}{\text{\# of words in the text}}$$

Word Recognition Rate: _____%

This student read _____% of the words in this selection correctly. Using this grade level of

text, the student reads at the _____ level.
　　　　　　　　　　　　　　　　(independent, instructional, frustrational)

Explanation of Text Difficulty Levels

Word Recognition Rate	Text Difficulty Level	Explanation
95%–100%	Independent	Easy enough to read alone comfortably; use for pleasure or at home
90%–94%	Instructional	Challenging enough to need help; use in the classroom for guided reading lessons
Below 90%	Frustrational	Too difficult for the student to read; more appropriate, depending on interest, for read-alouds by the teacher or parent.

(continued)

Figure 3.11 ■ Continued

2. Fluency Analysis: What is the student's rate of reading?

Time: _____ seconds   Words Per Minute: _____

Formula for WPM:

$$\frac{\text{\# of words in the text} \times 60}{\text{\# of seconds it took to read the text}}$$

Words Per Minute Rate Norms

First grade	54–79
Second grade	75–100
Third grade	100–124
Fourth grade	115–140
Fifth grade	125–150
Sixth grade	135–170

This student read _____ words per minute, which is/is not within the recommended range for his/her grade level.

3. Fluency Analysis: How many repetitions did the student make?

Number of repetitions: _____

Formula for Repetition Frequency:

$$\frac{\text{\# of words in the text}}{\text{\# of repetitions}}$$

This student made a repetition approximately every _____th word.

Figure 3.11 ■ Continued

4. Self-Regulation: How well does the student self-correct?

Formula for Self-Correction Rate:

$$\frac{\text{\# self-corrections}}{\text{\# of potential inaccurate word miscues}}$$

Potential incorrect word miscues = (# of inaccurate, substituted, or TA words) + (# of self-corrections)

This student self-corrected _____% of his/her potential inaccurate word miscues.

Anecdotal notes:

5. Miscue Analysis: How many of the student's miscues are semantically similar to the print?

Out of _____ incorrect or substituted word miscues, _____% were semantically similar to the print.

Formula for Percentage of Semantic Miscues:

$$\frac{\text{\# of semantic miscues}}{\text{\# of incorrect or substituted words}}$$

The spoken miscues that made sense within the context are shown below.

Printed text:	Incorrect or Substituted Word That is Semantically Similar:

(continued)

Figure 3.11 ■ Continued

---

6. Miscue Analysis: How many of the student's miscues are visually similar to the print?

Formula for Percentage of Visually Similar Miscues:

$$\frac{\text{\# of visually similar miscues}}{\text{\# of incorrect or substituted words}}$$

The spoken miscues that share graphic or phonological qualities with the words printed in text are shown below.

Printed text:	Incorrect or Substituted Word That is Visually Similar:

---

7. Retelling Analysis: How does the reader retell the story or informational text? (See the appropriate retelling checklist.)

Independent   Instructional   Frustrational

Figure 3.11 ■ Continued

8. Overall Results Reading Level

What is the reader-text match based on a combination of the Word Recognition Level and the Retelling Level?

The grade level of the text was _____.

The student's Word Recognition score was _____%. This is the _____ level.
(independent, instructional, frustrational)

The student's Retelling Level was _____ .
(independent, instructional, frustrational)

Overall Results Table
(Based on Leslie & Caldwell, 1990)

Word Recognition Level	Retelling Level	Overall Level for Reader-Text Match
Independent	Independent	Independent
Independent	Instructional	Instructional
Independent	Frustrational	Frustrational
Instructional	Independent	Instructional
Instructional	Instructional	Instructional
Instructional	Frustrational	Frustrational
Frustrational	Independent	Instructional
Frustrational	Instructional	Frustrational
Frustrational	Frustrational	Frustrational

The student's overall reading level is _____ .
(independent, instructional, frustrational)

Using Standards-Based Literacy Portfolios

> Miss Marlarkey is a good teacher. Usually she's really nice. But a couple of weeks ago she started acting a little weird. She started talking about THE TEST: The Instructional Performance Through Understanding test. I think Miss Malarkey said it was called the "I.P.T.U." test.
>
> ■ *Testing Miss Malarkey* (Finchler, 2000)

There is no doubt about it; standardized tests are important, and they are here to stay. If THE TEST makes you act "a little weird," perhaps it is because you realize the importance of assessing children's abilities with more than just one snapshot of their work. The demand to meet standards is real and perhaps justified. But attempting to capture your students' literacy growth with one set of numbers is unrealistic, and not reflective of their true abilities. Literacy portfolios can help.

Harris and Hodges define a portfolio as "a selected, usually chronological collection of a student's work that may be used to evaluate learning progress" (1995, p. 190). Therefore, a literacy portfolio is a collection of work that reflects the student's literacy abilities. According to Cohen and Wiener, "the primary purpose of a literacy portfolio is to improve literacy instruction by authentically assessing the child's development in reading and writing . . . An effective literacy portfolio enables the teacher to monitor a child's progress and affords ample opportunities to gain insights into strategies that the student uses" (2003, p. 90). By using standards-based literacy portfolios, you:

- Provide authentic assessment, which goes beyond the "one snapshot" picture of literacy provided by standardized tests.
- Collaborate with students and give them opportunities to reflect upon their work and choose their own evidence that they are learning.
- Have the opportunity to show caregivers tangible evidence of their children's learning.
- Are able to document how your classroom teaching aligns with state and local standards.
- Give students responsibility for their own learning by establishing criteria for inclusion of documents in the portfolio.
- Give students authentic learning opportunities by asking them to choose documents for the portfolio that were not constructed especially for the portfolio.

How is a Standards-Based Literacy Portfolio Organized?

It is generally understood that collecting student work is made easier and more efficient if there is an organizational system for doing so. According to Martin-Kniep, "When they are guided by standards, portfolios can provide a multidimensional view of students' development and achievement" (2003, p. 193). Portfolios can help you document your students' abilities to perform the standards that are part of your curriculum, allowing you to paint a broad picture of your students' literacy abilities which go beyond the snapshot that standardized testing provides. To make the documentation of literacy abilities efficient, it makes sense to help your students organize their portfolios so that they that house evidence of the most important components of literacy. The National Reading Panel (2000) outlined five areas of importance in reading: phonemic awareness, phonics, vocabulary, comprehension, and fluency. Shanahan (2003) explains that these five areas, however, are not the only important components, and Allington (2005) argues that a complete picture of reading includes its connection with writing, as well as the student's desire to read voluntarily. To reflect a comprehensive look at the literacy abilities of students in grades 1–8, I suggest organizing portfolios around the following areas: Phonics, Vocabulary, Comprehension, Fluency, Personal Reading, and Writing. Portfolios created at different grade levels may be organized differently; for example, in most cases, a middle school student's portfolio would not include documentation for phonics, while a third-grade student's portfolio would. Depending on the grade you teach, sections in your students' portfolios can be created so that they can house documents in these areas.

What Goes into the Standards-Based Portfolio?

Your students' literacy portfolios can contain any evidence of student learning; preferably, the work that goes into the portfolio is authentic and reflective of a standard or one of the important areas in reading. In order for the portfolios in your classroom to reflect true growth in student learning, it is important that your students have opportunities to reflect upon their work and choose their own documents for showing evidence of their learning. Many teachers find it necessary to delineate their students' portfolios to some extent, especially when both teacher and student are new to the experience of creating and using them (Martin-Kniep, 2003). You can specify the types of assignments and assessments that you want your students to include, and give them the opportunity to choose among several that they have completed. You can also specify chronological limits, such as telling students that they must enter one document per week. Documents for literacy portfolios might include: student writing samples; classroom assessments such as running records, repeated reading charts, and decoding checklists; goals; artwork; projects; surveys; literature responses; personal dictionaries; story maps; story frames; report frames; or letters.

To organize the portfolio, have your students create "sections" or "chapters" for each area that you want them to document. If you follow the plans suggested in this book, they will have six sections. At the beginning of the section, they should insert a

"Portfolio Cover Sheet." This sheet tells the reader of the student's portfolio about the types of documents included for that area. For example, at the beginning of the phonics section of the portfolio, your students' Portfolio Cover Sheet for phonics would contain statements such as: "This is what I put in my portfolio to show my ability to blend sounds." The student would then briefly describe the document and explain how it shows their abilities.

Additionally, you can ask students to include a table of contents, and a "personal" section that houses a self-portrait or photograph, an autobiography, and a statement or letter to the child written by caregivers or parents.

Documenting Literacy Abilities

The remaining material in this section will show you some of the possibilities for your students' literacy portfolios. For each of the six areas recommended for documentation, I offer several assessment activities you can use to help your students document their literacy abilities. Additionally, for each documented area, you'll see the Portfolio Cover Sheet for inclusion in the portfolio.

■ Phonics

The purpose of teaching phonics is to provide students with a tool for figuring out words they do not know. In order to accomplish that, they need to be able to do four things: recognize letter/sound relationships, blend the sounds represented by letters into the appropriate words, use words they know to figure out new words, and tackle unknown words independently. Each of these can be assessed with simple classroom assessment tools.

Letter/Sound Relationships and Blending

El Paso Phonics Survey.   In this assessment, the student is given a list of nonsense words that must be segmented by the sounds, and then blended to pronounce the entire word. You can find the test in the *Ekwall/Shanker Reading Inventory*, published by Allyn & Bacon (Shanker & Ekwall, 2000). The El Paso survey, which can be used with any grade level, assesses 90 phonics elements and indicates the point at which each element is expected to be known. For example, the scoring sheet indicates that single initial consonant sounds are expected to be known by the end of the first grade year. Advantages of using the El Paso Phonics Survey include: 1) It assesses children's abilities to blend phonic elements, and 2) Nonsense words are used, eliminating the possibility that the students will get items correct because they know the words by sight.

Classroom Decoding Check.   Created by first-grade teacher, Nancy Steider, (Steider, cited in Nettles, 2006), this classroom assessment tool can be produced and administered quickly. Steider creates a short list of nonsense words that contain the letters and sounds that the student has recently learned in class. The student must segment and blend the sounds, and then pronounce the list of words. For example, when shown the nonsense word *thuss*, the child would say, "thuh . . . uh . . . s-s-s- . . . thuss," and you would write the pronunciation that the child makes. To use this assessment in your classroom, create no more than 10 nonsense words that consist of phonetic patterns that your students have recently learned. This decoding check will determine your students' abilities to blend phonic elements, giving you a true picture of their decoding. Nonsense words eliminate the possibility of falsely positive results.

Using Known Words to Decode Unknown Words

Making Words Strategy. Cunningham and Cunningham (1992) offer this strategy as a way to help students learn new words based on familiar words. The teacher gives students letter cards and then tells them clues about words. Connect this strategy to classroom reading by using words and clues from children's books, such as, "Use three letters. Make a word that tells what the cat had on his head." As the students make progressively more difficult words, they rely on their knowledge of the easier words and build upon them. Then, after making words, students sort them into categories. In *A Handbook for Literacy: Instructional and Assessment Strategies K-8*, Antonacci and O'Callaghan (2006) provide a checklist to use in assessing students' abilities to generate words and sort them.

Word Families Book. Give your students a book of blank pages, and a rime for each page. They record word families by creating as many words as possible with different onsets. Assess each page with a rubric such as the one shown in Figure 4.1.

Figure 4.1 ■ Rubric for Creating Word Families

5	3	1
Student independently created all possible words for this rime.	Student independently created many possible words for this rime, with some nonsense words included.	Student independently created few, if any, possible words for this rime. Most, if not all, are nonsense words.
Student can say each of the words in this word family.	Student can say many of the words in this word family.	Student cannot say the words in this word family.

Decoding Unknown Words Independently

Visually Similar Miscues Analysis. During a running record, you can record the number of visually similar miscues the student makes. This analysis indicates the ways in which the student relies on letter/sound correspondences to figure out unknown words. See Figure 3.8 for the record form for this assessment.

The Names Test. In this classroom assessment, the teacher shows the student a list of unfamiliar names, and the student must call them out, as if taking roll in the classroom. In her book, *Phonics They Use,* Cunningham (2005) carefully configured this assessment to contain a list of names representing all vowel sounds, consonant sounds, and the most common combinations. If the child misses a name, this indicates that he or she is unfamiliar with a particular set of sounds and cannot yet adequately decode them. For example, if the student cannot pronounce the last name "Tweed," he or she may be having difficulty with the "tw" blend or the vowel combination "ee."

My List of Hard Words. The student keeps a list of words that are too difficult to decode while reading. The child checks off the words after they have been learned. Assess and record his or her ability to learn new words with the rubric shown in Figure 4.2.

Figure 4.2 ■ Rubric for List of Hard Words

5	3	1
Student uses list of words very consistently as he reads difficult text.	Student sometimes uses the list of words as he reads difficult text.	Student rarely, if ever, uses the list of words as he reads difficult text.

Figure 4.3 provides a checklist your students can complete and put in the portfolio to record their self-reflections of their abilities to use phonics.

Figure 4.3 ■ Portfolio Cover Sheet for Documenting Phonics Abilities

---

Portfolio Cover Sheet: Things I Can Do with Phonics

My name is _____ .

I can blend sounds.

This is what I put in my portfolio to show my ability to blend sounds:

Date: _____

_____

It shows that I can _____

_____ .

I can make new words out of words I already know.

This is what I put in my portfolio to show my ability to make new words:

Date: _____

_____

It shows that I can _____

_____ .

I can independently figure out words I don't know.

This is what I put in my portfolio to show that I can figure out words:

Date: _____

_____

It shows that I can _____

_____ .

■ Vocabulary

When your students "know" words and are able to call them their own, they are able to correctly define words, and use words appropriately in writing. Take a look at some ways to assess and document these types of vocabulary knowledge.

Defining Words. Students can keep blank journal booklets, or personal dictionaries, in which to record new words. Word entries must be defined in such a way that it is evident the student knows these things: what it is, what it is like, some examples of the word, and how to use it in writing. Students can illustrate their definitions (See Figure 4.4) and create stories (See Figure 4.5).

They can also use mnemonics to help them understand, remember, and use the word. For example, suppose your student needs to remember the word *finance*. This word sounds like "fine aunts." Thus, the student can picture some wealthy aunts, whose personal money holdings, or "finances," are quite good. Strategies such as the Concept of Word procedure (Schwartz & Raphael, 1985) and the Keyword Method (National Reading Panel, 2000; Pressley, Levin, & Delaney, 1982) can help students define words. Use the rubric shown in Figure 4.6 to assess your students' personal dictionaries.

Using Words Appropriately. An indication of how well students know words is their use of words in writing. To assess their word choices, you can use Trait #4 of the Writing Rubrics, shown in Section Two of this book. Figure 4.7 shows the Portfolio Cover Sheet for Vocabulary that your students can use to document their abilities in vocabulary knowledge and usage.

Figure 4.4

Undulate

Undulate means to move in waves or like a wave. Undulate comes from English and late Latin.

Here are some things that undulate:

People   Wheat   Grass

Figure 4.5

Bonanza

A bonanza is a rich source of wealth or profit. It is also a lucky find. Bonanza is a Spanish word.

If a genie gave me a billion dollars, that would be a bonanza. First I would build five dream houses around America. Then I would buy a private jet and put the rest of my money in the bank so I could get interest on my bonanza. Finally, when I got very old, I would give ninety percent of my money to charity.

Tom's Castle

Figure 4.6 ■ Rubric for Assessing Personal Dictionaries

5	3	1
The student enters the designated number of words per week in his dictionary.	The student enters at least half of the designated number of words per week in his dictionary.	The student enters less than half of the designated number of words per week in his dictionary.
The student defines all words correctly, using words that are his own.	The student defines some words correctly, using words that are his own.	The student defines few, if any, words correctly, using words that are his own.
The student can, for each of the words, explain what the word is like, using synonyms and examples.	The student can, for some of the words, explain what the word is like, using synonyms and examples.	For few, if any, of the words, the student explains what the word is like, using synonyms and examples.
The student correctly illustrates or provides graphics for all word definitions, indicating a thorough understanding of all words in the personal dictionary.	The student correctly illustrates or provides graphics for some word definitions, indicating an adequate understanding of some of the words in the personal dictionary.	The student correctly illustrates or provides graphics for few, if any, word definitions, indicating a poor understanding of most of the words in the personal dictionary.
The student appropriately uses many of these new words in his writing, as well as in conversations about books.	The student appropriately uses some of these new words in his writing, as well as in conversations about books.	The student appropriately uses few, if any, of these new words in his writing, as well as in conversations about books

Figure 4.7 ■ Portfolio Cover Sheet for Documenting Vocabulary Abilities

Portfolio Cover Sheet: Things I Can Do with Vocabulary

My name is _____ .

I can explain what words mean in my Personal Dictionary.

This is what I put in my portfolio to show my ability to tell what words mean:

Date: _____

_____

It shows that I can _____

_____

I can use new words in writing.

This is what I put in my portfolio in my portfolio to show my ability to use words in writing:

Date: _____

_____

It shows that I can _____

_____

■ Comprehension

Without comprehension, reading does not truly exist. Your students' ability to construct meaning from print is the key to their success as readers. It is important to think of comprehension as a process, rather than as a product, because there are many pieces to the puzzle of comprehension. Good readers do many things to help themselves comprehend, including:

1. Make logical predictions based on structure of text as well as prior experiences, and verify them while reading.
2. While reading, make inferences, which are interpretations of the print in which the reader applies the information given by the author to his own experiences.
3. While reading, visualize text with mental pictures.
4. When reading for information, generate self-questions to enable construction of meaning.

Figure 4.8 ■ Prediction Self-Assessment Sheet for Picture Books or Transition Books

Name: _____   Date: _____

Book: _____   Author: _____

Stop-point	What I predict will happen:	Why I am making this prediction:	Type of clue:	After reading, I found out:
Page: _____			Pictures Words My experiences What I know about the author	
Page: _____			Pictures Words My experiences What I know about the author	
Page: _____			Pictures Words My experiences What I know about the author	

1. When making predictions, I use this type of clue most often:

   Pictures   Words   My experiences   What I know about the author

2. I found out that when I make predictions, I _____ .

5. After reading fiction, identify all the story elements in a retelling.

6. After reading fiction, briefly summarize the story using as few details as possible.

Look now at ways to document your students' abilities in each of these areas of reading comprehension.

Making Predictions.   In the portfolio, students can document their abilities to make logical predictions using these prediction self-assessment sheets. Figure 4.8 provides a prediction self-assessment sheet that is for use with easy picture books, or transition books, such as *Frog and Toad All Year* (Lobel, 1976). The second self-assessment sheet (Figure 4.9) is to be used with chapter books, and enables your students to

Figure 4.9 ■ Prediction Self-Assessment Sheet for Chapter Books

Name: _____			Date: _____	
Book: _____		Author: _____		

Chapter	What I predict will happen in this chapter:	Why I am making this prediction:	Type of clue:	After reading, I found out:
			What I've read so far My experiences What I know about the author What I know about this type of book	
			What I've read so far My experiences What I know about the author What I know about this type of book	
			What I've read so far My experiences What I know about the author What I know about this type of book	

1. When making predictions, I use this type of clue most often:

   What I've read so far

   My experiences

   What I know about the author

   What I know about this type of book

3. I found out that when I make predictions when reading chapter books, I _____ .

Figure 4.10 ■ Prediction Self-Assessment Sheet Formats for Emerging Readers

Accordion-style Prediction Sheet:

My Prediction Title of Book: _____ My Name: _____	My prediction	My clues	What really happened

Booklet-style Prediction Sheet

My Prediction Booklet Title of Book: _____ My Name: _____	My prediction
My clues Pictures Words My Head	What really happened

show that they can process print in larger pieces of text and think about how they make predictions based on features of the text as well as prior knowledge. Finally, Figure 4.10 is designed for beginning, or emerging, readers. It can be created from a sheet of paper folded accordion-style, or in half to resemble a booklet. Students draw and label the responses.

Making Inferences. Block (2004) suggests that readers need to be able to interpret the author's meaning by applying information from the text to their own lives and introduces an assessment called "What Do We Need to Fill In?" (p. 205). To use this assessment, give students a paragraph that is somewhat ambiguous if it stands alone, outside the context of the entire book. Be sure not to tell them the title of the book from which the paragraph came. Examples of such paragraphs from several books of varying difficulty levels are shown in Figures 4.11–4.16. Students read the paragraphs, and then retell what they remember from the text. Next, they explain what is needed to make the passage complete for someone else to read. They verbalize this while you make notes. As students describe the "missing link," they need to be able to tell how this would make the passage more comprehensible.

For example, in the passage from *The Man Who Walked Between the Towers* (Gerstein, 2003), the student might say that the passage should explain what the wire is, and what the main character is doing on the wire. Block explains that when children explain what is needed for others to comprehend better, they are revealing what would help themselves understand better.

Figure 4.11 ■ Passage for Documentation of Making Inferences from *George and Martha Back in Town* by (Marshall, 1984)

> Martha climbed up the ladder.
> "Now what?" said George.
> "I'll go first," said Martha.
> And she jumped off.
> Martha caused quite a splash. Everyone was impressed.
> And no one noticed how George got down.

Retelling: Complete   Partial   Unsatisfactory

In order for someone else to understand this passage, it needs:

_____

_____

_____

_____

Figure 4.12 ■ Passage for Documentation of making inferences from *The Man Who Walked Between the Towers* (Gerstein, 2003)

> He even lay down to rest. The city and harbor spread beneath him. The sky surrounded him. Seagulls flew under and over. As long as he stayed on the wire he was free.

Retelling: Complete   Partial   Unsatisfactory

In order for someone else to understand this passage, it needs:

_____

_____

_____

_____

Figure 4.13 ■ Passage for Documentation of Making Inferences from *Tuck Everlasting* (Babbit, 1975, p. 41)

> "And we figured it'd be very bad if everyone knowed about that spring," said Mae. "We begun to see what it would mean." She peered at Winnie. "Do you understand, child? That water—it stops you right where you are. If you'd had a drink of it today, you'd stay a little girl forever. You'd never grow up, not ever."

Retelling: Complete   Partial   Unsatisfactory

In order for someone else to understand this passage, it needs:

_____

_____

_____

_____

Figure 4.14 ■ Passage for Documentation of Making Inferences from *Bud, Not Buddy* (Curtis, 1999, p. 80)

> I'd learned that it was best to be asleep before Momma finished the story because if she got done and I was still awake she'd always tell me what the story was about. I never told Momma, but that always ruint the fun of the story. Shucks, here I was thinking I was just hearing something funny about a fox or a dog and Momma spoilt it by telling me they were really lessons about not being greedy or not wishing for things you couldn't have.
>
> I took two more breaths and started thinking about the little hen that baked the bread. I heard, "'Not I,' said the pig. 'Not I,' said the goat. 'Not I,' said the big bad wolf," then woop, zoop, sloop . . . I was asleep.

Retelling: Complete   Partial   Unsatisfactory

In order for someone else to understand this passage, it needs:

_____

_____

_____

_____

Figure 4.15 ■ Passage for Documentation of Making Inferences from *Esperanza Rising* (Muñoz Ryan, 2000, p. 56)

Sadness and anger tangled in Esperanza's stomach as she thought of all that she was leaving: her friends and her school, her life as it once was, Abuelita. And Papa. She felt as though she was leaving him, too.

As if reading her mind, Mama said, "Papa's heart will find us wherever we go." Then Mama took a determined breath and headed toward the sprawling trees.

Esperanza followed but hesitated every few steps, looking back. She hated leaving, but how could she stay?

With each stride, Papa's land became smaller and smaller. She hurried after Mama, knowing that she might never come back to her home again, and her heart filled with venom for Tío Luis.

Retelling: Complete   Partial   Unsatisfactory

In order for someone else to understand this passage, it needs:

_____

_____

_____

Figure 4.16 ■ Passage for Documentation of Making Inferences from *The Secret School* (Avi, 2001, p. 108)

Her mother found Ida in bed. By the glowing light of a kerosene lamp she was rereading the school's frayed copy of *Great Orations by Great Men*.

"Ida, it's very late. You're pushing yourself too hard."

"What's the good of me being teacher?" Ida replied with anguish. "If everyone else passes the exams and I don't, it'll be the last time I ever teach."

"Honey, I'm sure you know more than you think."

"Ma, the exam is a couple of weeks away, but I have no idea what's in it. I have to know *everything*."

"Honey, I don't want you getting sick. Won't be good for anything then."

"I'll be a whole lot sicker if I don't get to high school."

Mrs. Bidson sighed and retreated down the ladder.

Retelling: Complete   Partial   Unsatisfactory

In order for someone else to understand this passage, it needs:

_____

_____

Figure 4.17 ■ Checklist for Visualizing Stories

The student can think about:

☐ Characters—How do they look? _____

_____

☐ Setting—What does it look like? _____

_____

☐ Things that happen—How do the characters look when they do things? _____

_____

Figure 4.18 ■ Checklist for Visualizing Nonfiction

The student obtains clues from:

☐ Descriptive words _____

☐ Comparisons to things already known _____

☐ Photographs _____

☐ Maps _____

☐ Charts _____

Visualizing.   Children seem to be able to readily make mind pictures to help them remember what they have read (Sadoski & Paivio, 2004). Moreover, visualizing personalizes the act of reading, because visual imagery is dependent upon the reader's experiences and personal outlook. Visualizing is also related to comprehension; thus, it makes sense to teach children to make mental pictures as they read, and to assess their ability to do so.

Provide students a passage that has no pictures, and ask them to complete one of these sentences:

"If I were illustrating this passage, I would draw . . ."

"The mind movie that is going on in my head right now shows . . ."

"I can see this, even when I close my eyes. In my mind picture, I see . . ."

Have students insert the passage and the sentence completion in the portfolio. Then, assess their ability to use clues with the checklists shown in Figures 4.17 and 4.18. Make notes where appropriate.

Metacognition.   Metacognition is the ability of students to monitor their own thinking while they read. Good readers are able to do this; poor readers are not. Below are five ways to document your students' abilities to monitor their reading.

Running Records.   The running record (Clay, 1985, 2000) is an excellent way to record students' reading behaviors. Section Three of this book contains forms for recording information gained from the running record. As shown in the Self-Regulation Mini-Assessment in Figure 3.6, the self-correction rate is indicative of the student's ability to recognize his or her oral reading errors and correct them without help. If you want to document a student's ability to correct his or her own errors while reading, have the child read short passages aloud to you over a period of time—perhaps one a week for a month. Record the self-correction rate each time and plot these scores on a graph. Insert the graph in the portfolio as a measure of self-regulation.

Think Alouds.   To use a think-aloud assessment, ask the student to read a piece of text. At stop-points that you have marked, ask the student to tell you what he or she is thinking about while reading. Record these think-aloud statements on the Think Aloud Record sheet shown in Figure 4.19. Categorize the statements by matching

Figure 4.19 ■ Think-Aloud Record Sheet

Think-Aloud Record

Stop-point	Page #	Student's think-aloud notes	Types of reading processes
		_____ _____	
		_____ _____	
		_____ _____	
		_____ _____	

Types of Reading Processes Revealed by Thinking Aloud

1. The student is attempting to figure out a word that gives him or her difficulty.
2. The student is recalling background knowledge to aid in comprehension.
3. The student is looking for information about characters or story.
4. The student is looking for information about the topic of the nonfiction selection.
5. The student is making predictions about the characters' actions or the events of the story.
6. The student is making predictions about the information he or she will find out.
7. The student is generating self-questions about the characters or story.
8. The student is generating self-questions about the information presented by the author.
9. The student is relating to the text on a personal level.

them to the Types of Reading Processes chart shown at the bottom of Figure 4.19. Next to each think-aloud statement, write the corresponding number of the reading process.

For example, suppose Cheyenne, a second grader, is reading *The Old Man and His Door* (Soto, 1996). Her teacher asks her to stop on the page where the old man is bathing his dog Coco while his wife attempts to give him instructions as she is leaving for a party. Just as Coco runs away from him and he's running around the yard trying to catch him, the man's wife yells to him to bring a pig to the barbeque. At this point, Cheyenne stops and says, "I don't know how to pronounce this word. I know it's Spanish. I think it's '*el pu- er- co.*' I think it means 'the pig,' because that's what the wife says in English in the last sentence." The teacher records the following in the first row of the chart:

Stop-point	Page #	Student's think-aloud notes	Types of reading processes
1	fifth page	Not sure how to pronounce word. Knows it's in Spanish. Attempts to say it. "I think it means the pig. . . that's what the wife says."	1, 3

You can ask students to include these charts in their portfolios to document their think-alouds.

Metacognition Strategy Index.   The Metacognition Strategy Index, or the MSI, created by Schmitt (1990) measures readers' awareness of strategies to use when their comprehension breaks down. The MSI is a 25-item multiple choice survey that explores what readers do before, during, and after they read stories. Directions for scoring, as well as reliability information, are provided in the March 1990 edition of *The Reading Teacher.*

Survey of Fix-up Strategies.   Using a set of sentence completions, the Survey of Fix-up Strategies, shown in Figure 4.20, asks students to explain how they correct themselves when reading mistakes or comprehension roadblocks occur. You can have students complete this survey at different times in the school year to get a long-term picture of their metacognitive awareness.

Figure 4.20 ■ Survey of Fix-up Strategies for Comprehending

When I come to a paragraph that I don't understand, I _____

_____ .

When I come to a sentence that confuses me, I _____

_____ .

When my mind wanders, I _____ .

The author I think is easiest to understand is _____ , because

_____ .

The type of book that I think is easiest to understand is _____ , because

_____ .

The reading ability that I want to improve most is _____ , because

_____ .

Collection of Passages.   Finally, your students can collect passages that have challenged them and write about the coping mechanisms they use to understand them. As they read, tell them to mark difficult words, sentences, or paragraphs with sticky notes. Later, after misconceptions are clarified and students have used strategies to enable their comprehension, have them add entries to a journal called "My Journal of Ways to Comprehend," using the format shown in Figure 4.21.

Self-Questioning.   Nonfiction text often demands more attention than fiction because of its sophisticated vocabulary, students' relative inexperience with the topic, and its remarkable difference in structure from fictional stories. Good readers are always asking questions. An indication of the reader's ability to process nonfiction text meaningfully is his or her ability to generate questions while reading (Palincsar & Brown, 1984). When your students can actively participate in interacting with the text and in satisfying their own curiosity as they read, they are processing print beyond merely reading words. Figure 4.22 shows a survey that your students can use to keep track of their self-questioning efforts.

Figure 4.21 ■ Ways to Comprehend Journal

This is a word that gave me difficulty: _____ . Here's why: This is what I did to fix it up: Date:	This is a sentence that gave me difficulty: *[Cut and paste a photocopy of the sentence, or write the sentence here.]* Here's why: This is what I did to fix it up: Date:
This is a paragraph that gave me difficulty: *[Cut and paste a photocopy of the paragraph here.]* Here's why: This is what I did to fix it up: Date:	This is a book that gave me difficulty: Title: Author: Here's why: This is what I did to fix it up: Date:

Figure 4.22 ■ Self-Assessment Survey for Self-Questioning While Reading Nonfiction

When I read nonfiction, I ask myself questions.

- I ask myself a question about the title.

5	4	3	2	1
Always				Never

- I ask myself a question about the author.

5	4	3	2	1
Always				Never

- I ask myself questions about headings and subheadings.

5	4	3	2	1
Always				Never

- I ask myself questions about pictures or photographs that I wonder about.

5	4	3	2	1
Always				Never

- I ask myself questions about maps and charts that interest me or give me ideas.

5	4	3	2	1
Always				Never

- I ask myself questions about vocabulary that is highlighted.

5	4	3	2	1
Always				Never

- I ask myself questions about things I already know about the topic.

5	4	3	2	1
Always				Never

Figure 4.23 ■ Writing a Summary in Just Four Sentences

Beginning of Story

Character is *where.*

The story takes place *when.*

Middle of Story

Character's problem is _____
_____ .

End of story

The problem is solved when _____
_____ .

Summarizing. When students summarize, they tell only the bare essentials of the text. Summarizing is shorter and less detailed than a retelling of the text, and is an important way of showing evidence of comprehension (Duke & Pearson, 2002; National Reading Panel, 2000). Children often want to retell, rather than summarize, so that they can include all the events, characters, and character traits (Harvey & Goudvis, 2000). Summarizing requires them to make decisions about only the most essential information about a story. Glazer (1998) recommends the three sentence story for students who have difficulty writing, I recommend adapting this strategy for summarizing what was read. Figure 4.23 shows a frame for this summary, which students can include in their portfolios.

Figure 4.24 ■ Identifying Story Elements and Retelling

Introduction Did I begin with an introduction? _____	
Beginning Characters Setting	Did I tell whom the story is about? _____ Did I tell where the story happens? _____ Did I tell when the story happens? _____
Middle Problem Events	Did I tell about the character's problem or what the character wants? _____ Did I tell about each of the events that happen because of this? _____
End Resolution	Did I tell how the problem was solved? _____ Did I tell how the story ends? _____
Conclusion Did I tell what I think of the story? _____	

Retelling.   Retelling is different from answering questions after reading; students' ability to retell a story reflects their ability to understand and recall the elements of story. Figure 4.24 shows a retelling checklist that students can use and insert in their portfolios.

Figure 4.25 shows the Cover Sheet students can fill out to explain the types of documents they use in their portfolio to showcase their comprehension abilities.

Fluency

Most teachers can recognize a fluent reader when they hear one. These readers read quickly, accurately, expressively, and with comprehension (National Reading Panel, 2000; Johns & Bergland, 2002, Samuels, 2002). They sound good when they read, and the reading makes sense to their listeners as well as to themselves. Samuels (2004) tells us that when the emerging reader reaches the point at which he or she is able to recognize words quickly and simultaneously comprehend the message, the reading is fluent. This means that the child can read with accuracy and speed, without the need to stop and decode single words. Fluency, then, allows the child to devote his or her efforts to comprehending the print. There are several ways that your students can document their fluency abilities.

Figure 4.25 ■ Portfolio Cover Sheet for Documenting Comprehension Abilities

---

Portfolio Cover Sheet: Ways I Can Show My Comprehension

My name is _____ .

I can make predictions.

This is what I put in my portfolio to show my ability to make predictions:

Date: _____

_____

This is what I did: _____

_____ .

I can make inferences. This means that I can figure out the author's meaning even when it is not written.

This is what I put in my portfolio to show my ability to make inferences:

Date: _____

_____

This is what I did: _____

_____ .

I can visualize text. This means that I can make pictures in my head about the words on the page.

This is what I put in my portfolio to show my ability to visualize:

Date: _____

_____

This is what I did: _____

_____ .

I can make up questions on my own.

This is what I put in my portfolio to show my ability to create questions:

Date: _____

_____

This is what I did: _____

_____ .

I can retell the story elements of a story.

This is what I put in my portfolio to show my ability to retell:

Date: _____

_____

This is what I did: _____

_____ .

I can briefly summarize a story.

This is what I put in my portfolio to show my ability to summarize:

Date: _____

_____

This is what I did: _____

_____ .

■ Charts for Accuracy and Speed

In Section Three, you saw some assessment tools that you can use in the classroom to discover a variety of things about your readers. Among other things, the Classroom Mini-Assessments can help you determine the accuracy of your students' word recognition (WR score), as well as the number of words per minute that they can read (WPM score). Both of these assessments are indicative of your students' fluency abilities. To document this, your students can keep charts of these scores, collected over a period of time, using repeated readings of the same text. Two such charts are shown in Figures 4.26 and 4.27.

■ Oral Reading Collections

One of the ways to encourage fluent reading is to ask your students to read aloud to others for enjoyment. There are many strategies that are helpful, such as Radio Reading, Readers' Theater, and Choral Reading (Opitz & Rasinski, 1998). All of these involve using excerpts from children's literature. Poetry Parties (Nettles, 2006) give your students the opportunity to choose favorite poems, practice reading them aloud, and share them with their families and classmates in a relaxed setting. To improve comprehension of students who need help with "culturally sensitive text," Block (2004, p.192) suggests that teachers use riddles, jokes, and trade books that

Figure 4.26 ■ Chart for Tracking the Student's WPM with Repeated Readings of the Same Passage.

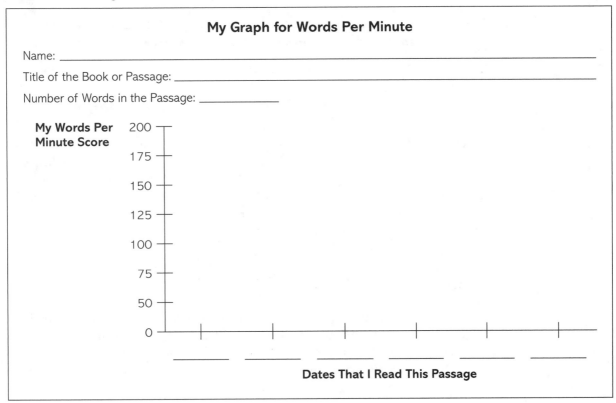

Figure 4.27 ■ Chart for Tracking Number of Word Recognition Errors Using Repeated Readings over Time

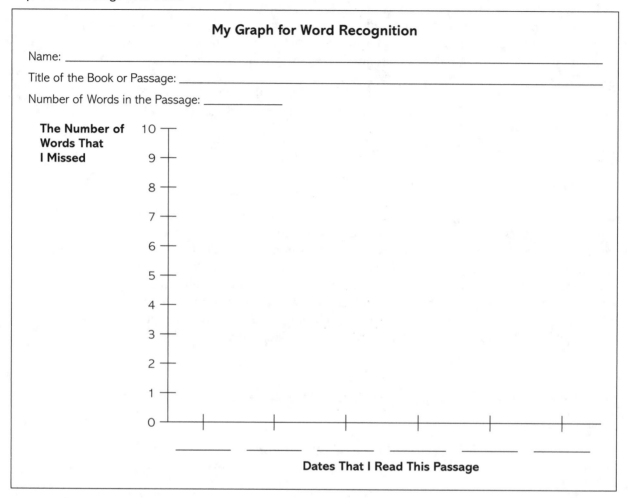

describe children's hobbies, and ask students to listen to these texts on tape, which increases their abilities to comprehend the text. These texts can also be used to help students develop oral reading fluency. After becoming familiar with these excerpts, they can read aloud to a tape recorder or to their peers. To document their work with fluency, you can ask students to collect poems, quotations, passages, riddles, and jokes and insert them in the portfolio.

■ Tape, Check, Chart

To document your students' growing competence in accuracy, Johns and Berglund suggest a strategy called Tape, Check, Chart (2002, p. 59). Using audiotape, students read aloud a passage of "appropriate difficulty" and record it. After reading, they listen to themselves and follow along with a photocopy of the passage. At each miscue (any deviation from the text), students mark a checkmark. They repeat this procedure two times, so that they have three recordings of their oral readings. Each time, they count their own miscues, and each time, they should see the number of miscues decrease. Johns and Berglund (2002) provide a chart, or you can use the one that I have adapted, shown in Figure 4.28.

To explain the documents that they have used to show evidence of fluency, your students can use the Cover Sheet shown in Figure 4.29.

Figure 4.28 ■ Adapted Chart for Tape, Check, Chart

Tape, Check, Chart	
Title of Passage or Book: _____	
Date:	**Number of Checkmarks**
Taped recording #1	
Taped recording #2	
Taped recording #3	

Figure 4.29 ■ Portfolio Cover Sheet for Documenting Fluency Abilities

Portfolio Cover Sheet: Things I Can Do to Show Reading Fluency

My name is _____ .

I can read quickly.

This is what I put in my portfolio to show my ability to read at an appropriate speed.

Date: _____

_____

This is what I did: _____

_____ .

I can read accurately.

This is what I put in my portfolio to show my ability to read accurately.

Date: _____

_____

This is what I did: _____

_____ .

I can read with expression.

This is what I put in my portfolio to show my ability to read with expression.

Date: _____

_____

This is what I did: _____

_____ .

Personal Reading

Standards-based instruction and high stakes testing might produce higher test scores. Sadly, another product of this current trend is likely to be reluctant readers. Yet, teachers who know that teaching is more than following a script also know that a huge part of their responsibility is to encourage their students to read voluntarily. The literacy portfolio is an excellent tool for helping students document the amount of reading they do. Figures 4.30 and 4.31 are reading logs for this purpose (N. Steider, personal communication, May 1, 2006). Additionally, your students can put response journals in this section. There are several ways to use these journals, such as dialogue journal responses, double-entry journals, point of view entries, sharing quotations, and stating opinions (Nettles, 2006, pp. 446–452). Cover sheets can be created for any of these entries that you choose.

Writing

In the second section of this book, you saw some rubrics that enable you to assess your students' writing abilities in six areas: ideas, organization, voice, word choice, sentence fluency, and conventions. Ask your students to submit written pieces on a regular basis (perhaps weekly or bi-weekly), which have been assessed on at least one of the traits listed above. They can use the Portfolio Cover Sheet, shown in Figure 4.32, to explain their documentation.

Figure 4.30 ■ Personal Reading Log for Early Readers

Date of First Reading	Title	Author	Number of Pages	Reading Level	Tally of Times Read	Rating (Circle number of stars)
						★ ★ ★ ★ ★
						★ ★ ★ ★ ★
						★ ★ ★ ★ ★
						★ ★ ★ ★ ★
						★ ★ ★ ★ ★
						★ ★ ★ ★ ★
						★ ★ ★ ★ ★
						★ ★ ★ ★ ★
						★ ★ ★ ★ ★

My goal for number of books read this month: _____

Figure 4.31 ■ Personal Reading Log for Older Readers

Date Started	Title	Author	Number of Pages	Number of Chapters	Date Finished	Rating (Circle number of stars)
						★ ★ ★ ★ ★ ★
						★ ★ ★ ★ ★ ★
						★ ★ ★ ★ ★ ★
						★ ★ ★ ★ ★ ★
						★ ★ ★ ★ ★ ★
						★ ★ ★ ★ ★ ★
						★ ★ ★ ★ ★ ★
						★ ★ ★ ★ ★ ★
						★ ★ ★ ★ ★ ★

My goal for number of books read this month: _____

Figure 4.32 ■ Portfolio Cover Sheet for Documenting Fluency Abilities

Portfolio Cover Sheet: Things I Can Do to Show My Writing Abilities

My name is _____ .

I can use new ideas in my writing.

This is what I put in my portfolio to show my ability to use new ideas.

Date: _____

_____

This is what I did: _____

_____

_____ .

I can organize my writing well.

This is what I put in my portfolio to show my ability to organize my writing.

Date: _____

_____

This is what I did: _____

_____

_____ .

I can write with appropriate and interesting voice.

This is what I put in my portfolio to show I can write with voice.

Date: _____

_____

This is what I did: _____

_____

_____ .

I can choose words well when I write.

This is what I put in my portfolio to show my ability to choose words.

Date: _____

_____

This is what I did: _____

_____

_____ .

(continued)

Figure 4.32 ■ Continued

I can use sentences well when I write.

This is what I put in my portfolio to show my ability to use sentences.

Date: _____

_____

This is what I did: _____

_____

_____ .

I follow the grammar and spelling rules when I write.

This is what I put in my portfolio to show my ability to use correct grammar and spelling.

Date: _____

_____

This is what I did: _____

_____

_____ .

Phonics Mini-Lessons: Understanding the Nature of Words

> The world has changed in a million ways. That is why I have always tried to teach children something that would be useful no matter what. But after all these years, words are still important. Words are still needed by everyone.
>
> ■ *Frindle* (Clements, 1996)

When teaching reading, you must help children know the "whole" as well as the "parts." In other words, you will teach children about books, stories, articles, websites and chapters; however, you also must teach children about words, as did Mrs. Granger, the teacher so beautifully portrayed by Andrew Clements in *Frindle* (1996). This special section is designed to help you remember—or learn for the first time— the elements of English words. In particular, you will learn the important components of phonics. If phonics is new to you, or if your memory of phonetic elements and generalizations is fuzzy, the following 14 mini-lessons will help you practice identifying important components of phonics elements that will aid your instruction. Each contains brief instruction and a quiz to assess your learning. If you are well-versed in the nature of words, this will be a review for you, and you may wish to skim it, or pick and choose the mini-lessons that suit you best. Lessons in this section cover:

1: Consonants

2: Vowels

3: Y and W as Vowels

4: R-controlled Vowels

5: Vowel Digraphs

6: Vowel Diphthongs

7: Schwa

8: Hard and Soft *C* and *G*

9: The CVC or Closed Syllable Pattern

10: The CVCe Pattern

11: The CVVC Pattern

12: The CV or Open Syllable Pattern

13: Syllabication Patterns

14: Words with Affixes

Phonics is the understanding of the relationship between letters and the sounds that they represent. When you use phonics to determine an unknown word, you attempt to orally or silently pronounce the word, based on what you know about the combination of letters that you see in that word. Phonics is one of the tools that help you make reasonable guesses about the words you see on a page.

You might be wondering, "Why do I need to learn this? Why is it important to know a digraph from a diphthong or a consonant blend from a consonant digraph?" There are three reasons.

First, knowing the make-up of words helps you determine what is important to teach when making decisions about the "parts" of reading. Ultimately, these decisions should be yours, and the only way to make decisions professionally is by being informed.

Second, a very pragmatic reason for understanding phonics is that you may encounter this information on tests required by your state or university. Keep in mind, however, that knowledge of the elements of phonics is not as important as your ability to teach your students how to use letter/sound relationships wisely as they tackle unknown words. In fact, according to Cunningham (2005), "Although some studies have reported that many teachers fail such tests of phonics knowledge, there are no studies that demonstrate that teachers who actually pass such tests actually can and do teach more effectively or even teach phonics more effectively" (p. 196).

Third, these are the tools of our trade. Just as every other profession uses labels and terms, teachers need to be able to describe the parts of reading. In order to converse with colleagues and with parents, teachers need a common term for letter combinations, sounds, and phonetic elements. It is not necessary to teach all of these terms to children, as long as the concepts underlying them are taught in a way that leads to meaningful decoding. "Teachers need the labels; readers need to read!" (Rasinski & Padak, 2001, p. 13)

Most of these mini-lessons present phonics concepts in an inductive manner. To introduce a new phonetic element or generalization, the mini-lesson shows you several example words that contain the same element or that have a similar spelling pattern. Based on the examples, you can determine how the words are alike, and then draw conclusions about the phonetic elements or make generalizations on your own. Finally, at the end of each lesson, you will see a brief self-quiz to check yourself on how well you remember the lesson, and a review of the concepts that you learned.

Common terms and definitions are necessary as you proceed. Phonics is the relationship between letters and words; therefore, you will see several terms that refer to parts of words, letters, or sounds. Letters, of course, are those symbols from the alphabet that we all are familiar with, and depending upon their placement in the spelling of a word, are written representations of sounds. A *grapheme* is another word for the written representation of sounds; however, a grapheme can consist of more than one letter. For example, the first sound that is heard in the word "share" is represented by the grapheme "sh." The word *phoneme* is used to connote the smallest unit of sound in a word. For example, in the word "hit," each letter represents a sound. Therefore, the word "hit" contains three graphemes, and three phonemes. In another example, the word "meat" contains three graphemes: "m," "ea," and "t." Moreover, because the "ea" in the middle of the word represents only one sound, it contains only three phonemes. A phoneme is indicated in many books on phonics and reading instruction with this symbol: / /. Therefore, when you see this symbol, keep in mind that a sound, not necessarily a letter, is indicated. For example, /b/ represents the sound "buh," as in "balloon." In another example, /s/ represents the hissing sound you hear at the beginning of the word "city." Likewise, you'll see vowel phonemes represented in professional literature in a couple of different ways. The "short" vowel sounds, such as the one heard in the word "cat," are often shown in teaching materials as "ă." However, in this book, short vowels are represented in this manner: /a/. The "long" vowel sounds, such as the one heard in the word *ate*, are represented in this book like this: /ā/.

Now, turn the page for the first mini-lesson. Let's begin!

Mini-Lesson 1: Consonants

Consonants are letters. In the English alphabet, there are twenty-one consonants: *b, c, d, f, g, h, j, k, l, m, n, p, q, r, s, t, v, w, x, y,* and *z.* The *w* and the *y* can also function as vowels. The most predictable sounds of all of the consonants are shown below.

Figure ML1.1 ■ Predictable Single Consonant Sounds

The letter...	represents the phoneme(s)...
b	/b/ as in *bear.*
c	/k/ as in *cat,* or /s/ as in *city*
d	/d/ as in *dog*
f	/f/ as in *fox*
g	/g/ as in *go,* or /j/ as in *geography*
h	/h/ as in *hat*
j	/j/ as in *jam*
k	/k/ as in *kitchen*
l	/l/ as in *lion*
m	/m/ as in *man*
n	/n/ as in *nice*
p	/p/ as in *pickle*
q, when paired with the letter *u*	a blend of the phonemes /k/ and /w/, as in *queen,* or /k/ sound, as in *opaque*
r	/r/ as in *run*
s	/s/ as in *sun* also /zh/, as in *pleasure,* or /sh/, as *tension*
t	/t/ as in *turtle*
v	/v/ as in *violin*
w, when at the beginning of a word or syllable	/w/ as in *well.*
x, when at the end of a word or syllable	/k/ and /s/ blended together, as in *fox;* also /z/ as in *anxiety*
y, when at the beginning of a word or syllable	/y/ as in *yellow*
z	/z/ as in *zoo*

Consonant Blends. Now, let's look at combinations of consonants. See if you can draw some conclusions on your own. Study the following list of words from the book, *Spot's First Picnic*, by Eric Hill (1987). Pronounce the words to yourself.

Word List 1

Spot	sticky	crash	trouble	cloudy	splash
stepping	stream	branch	slippery	Steve	crossed
stones	grass	dry	climbed	started	tricks
dry	friends	small	tree		

As you look at these words, notice that each begins with two or three consonants. When pronouncing them, you may have noticed that you can hear the sound represented by each consonant at the beginning of the word.

A **consonant blend** (sometimes called a *consonant cluster*) is a combination of two or three consonants that are adjacent in the same syllable. Each of the consonants represents its own sound and this sound is heard in the blend. Examples of consonant blends are: *bl* as in *blue, cr* as in *crown, str* as in *street, gr* as in *green, tw* in *twilight* and *scr* as in *scream*. Eldredge (2004) identified 27 consonant blends that occur most often at the beginning of words in children's reading materials, in order of frequency. These are shown in Figure ML1.2.

Figure ML1.2 ■ Common Initial Consonant Blends

1. *st* as in *sticky* and *stare*	15. *sl* as in *slick* and *sleep*
2. *pr* as in *pretty* and *pride*	16. *sw* as in *sweet* and *swim*
3. *tr* as in *tree* and *trick*	17. *sm* as in *smell* and *smog*
4. *gr* as in *green* and *grab*	18. *sc* as in *scatter* and *scale*
5. *pl* as in *please* and *play*	19. *thr* as in *throw* and *three*
6. *cl* as in *clown* and *clear*	20. *sk* as in *skate* and *skunk*
7. *cr* as in *crinkle* and *crash*	21. *gl* as in *glad* and *glitter*
8. *str* as in *street* and *strange*	22. *tw* as in *twilight* and *twine*
9. *br* as in *brown* and *bring*	23. *scr* as in *scream* and *scratch*
10. *dr* as in *drive* and *drag*	24. *spr* as in *spray* and *spring*
11. *sp* as in *spin* and *spill*	25. *sn* as in *sniff* and *snow*
12. *fl* as in *fly* and *flag*	26. *spl* as in *splash* and *split*
13. *fr* as in *friend* and *frozen*	27. *shr* as in *shrimp* and *shrug*
14. *bl* as in *black* and *blue*	

A consonant blend can also occur at the end of a word, such as the *-nd* blend in the word *and*. Some other common final consonant blends are: *-nt* as in *sent, -mp* as in *stamp*, and *-nk* as in *link*.

Consonant Digraphs. There is a consonant combination that is different from a blend or cluster. Word List 2 provides additional words from *Spot's First Picnic* (Hill, 1987). Notice the appearance of the words. Then pronounce them and think about the first phoneme in each.

Word List 2

they	then	shouted	charge	there	where
third	that	who	while	when	shower
shake	whoops	what	chuckled	thanks	

What do you notice about the beginning consonant phonemes in these words? These consonant sounds are different from the ones in Word List 1, because you hear only one consonant sound. When two or more consonants are grouped together in a syllable, and they represent a single sound, the combination is called a **consonant digraph**. Most of the time, the phoneme is a unique sound not represented by any other letter, such as the /sh/ sound in the word *shake*. However, there is another consonant digraph to know about, which represents the phoneme we usually associate with the letter "f": "ph" as in *phonics*.

Take a look back at Word List 1 and Figure ML1.2. Two consonant blends, #19 and #27, are a little different from the rest: *thr* as in *three*, and *shr* as in *shrug*. Both of these consonant blends are a combination of a digraph (which has one sound) and another consonant (which has one sound), thus creating a consonant blend of two sounds. Figure ML1.3 shows the common consonant digraphs.

Figure ML1.3 ■ Common Consonant Digraphs

- The letters "th" can represent the phoneme /th/, as in *thick*, and /th/ as in *that*.
- The letters "ch" usually represent the phoneme /ch/ as in *chicken*. Sometimes the "ch" represents /sh/ as in *machine*, or /k/ as in *chemistry*.
- The letters "sh" usually represent the phoneme /sh/ as in *shoe*.
- The letters "wh" usually represent the phoneme /hw/ as in *white*. Sometimes the letters "wh" represent the phoneme /h/ as in *who*.
- The letters ph always represent the phoneme /f/ as in *phonics*.

Silent Consonants. Still another type of consonant combination is somewhat common in the English language. Look at the words in Word List 3 and draw a conclusion about them.

Word List 3

knock   write   knit   wren   eight   sight   thought   through

As you can see, there is a consonant combination in each of these words, too. However, these words are different from those in the other lists in this lesson. The phoneme represented by the letters "kn" in *knock* is /n/ and the phoneme represented by "wr" in *write* is /r/. In the words *eight* and *thought*, the *gh* says nothing at all. These words contain consonant combinations that have silent letters. (Keep in mind, however, that the *gh* combination can also represent the phoneme /f/, as in *cough*. This only occurs at the end of a word.)

To review what you have learned, take your first self-quiz.

Self-Quiz for Mini-Lesson 1

Test yourself. In each of the following, which one does not belong? Tell why.

A. flutter, thing, spangle   _____

B. spin, sherry, chocolate   _____

C. strap, slim, shot   _____

D. knee, this, wrote   _____

E. night, slow, drive   _____

F. shrug, that, drill   _____

G. eight, sigh, tough   _____

Review for Mini-Lesson 1

In Mini-Lesson 1, you learned that:

1. A consonant blend or cluster is a combination of two or three consonants in the same syllable, in which both of the phonemes represented by the consonants are pronounced.

2. A consonant digraph is a combination of consonants in the same syllable, which represent a single consonant phoneme. Most of the time the phoneme is unique, such as the /sh/ phoneme in *share*. However, the *ph* digraph represents the phoneme usually associated with letter *f*, as in the word *phonics*.

3. Sometimes a consonant blend consists of a digraph, plus a single consonant, such as the *shr* in the word *shrimp*. The /sh/ is a phoneme, blended with the /r/, creating a blend of two consonant phonemes.

4. Some consonant combinations, such as *wr, kn,* and *gh* contain a letter that represents no sound, or a silent letter.

5. Sometimes, the same letter combination serves two functions. Notice that "gh" represents the /f/ phoneme as in *rough*, and they are silent letters in the word *weight*.

Mini-Lesson 2: Vowels

The English alphabet contains five pure vowel letters that represent vowel sounds, or vowel phonemes. These letters are: *a, e, i, o,* and *u.* The two most common sounds represented by the vowels are called "long" and "short" vowel sounds. The next few exercises will help to refresh your memory of the sounds these letters represent.

Long Vowels.   Look at the words in Word List 4. Each of the words, or a derivative of the word, is in the reprint edition of the classic, *The Tale of Peter Rabbit* by Beatrix Potter (1987). Say them out loud to yourself. All of the words have a phoneme in common. Can you identify the phoneme? Try to focus on the *sound* of the word.

Word List 4

tail   gate   ate   frame   rake   safe   tablespoonful   taken   straightaway

Did you say that all of these words have a vowel sound like the sound of the letter *a*? This phoneme is called the long *a* vowel and is represented with the /ā/ symbol.

Now look at Word Lists 5 to 8. Again, most of the words come from *The Tale of Peter Rabbit.* Each of these lists consists of words that have long vowel sounds in them. Identify the vowel phoneme that is common in each list.

Word List 5

Peter	tree	fields	squeezed	beans	meet
knees	thief	each	tea	underneath	least
speaking	peas	leaving	sneezed	wheelbarrow	three

Word List 6

pie	five	might	excitement	hide
tried	fright	time	alive	fortnight

Word List 7

go	potatoes	overheard	stone	close
hoeing	scarecrow	rabbit-hole	dose	clothes

Word List 8

cucumber   beautiful

The way to remember the long vowel phoneme is that this is the sound of the letter itself. For example, the long sound of *e* sounds like *he.* All five vowels have a long phoneme. Keep in mind, though, that sometimes the long vowel phoneme is not represented by that same vowel. For example, the word *eight* contains the /ā/ phoneme, but it is not represented by an *a.* Instead, the *ei* letters (or graphemes) represent the phoneme in this word.

You can remember these phonemes by associating a word or name with each of them (Cunningham, 2004). One helpful way for children to remember them is to remember storybook characters whose names contain this vowel phoneme. These names are shown in Figure ML2.1.

Figure ML2.1 ■ Long Vowel Phoneme Mnemonics

- /a/ as in *Jake* from *Jake Baked the Cake* (Hennessey, 1990)
- /e/ as in *teeny* from *The Teeny Tiny Woman* (Galdone, 1984)
- /i/ as in *Ira* from *Ira Sleeps Over* (Waber, 1972)
- /o/ as in *Rosie* from *Rosie's Walk* (Hutchins, 1968)
  or /o/ as in *Oma* from *Oma's Quilt* (Bourgeouis, 2001)
- /u/ as in *Trudy* from *Tell Me a Trudy* (Segal, 1977)

Short Vowels.   To find out more about vowel sounds, look at the words in Word List 9. Each is from the book, *Mike Mulligan and His Steam Shovel* by Virginia Lee Burton (1939). Say them out loud to yourself to discover the phoneme that these words have in common.

Word List 9

that	landing	faster	had	gasoline	sad
gravel	had	added	rather	bang	crash
slam	apple	janitor	caterpillars		

What vowel phoneme do you hear in each of these words? This is the sound of *a* that you hear in the word *cat* or *van*. It is called the short *a*, or /a/.

Read the words in the next four word lists. Say them slowly to yourself and see if you can hear the vowel phoneme in them.

Word List 10

red	never	cellars	better	seven	electric
left	every	them	together	well	telegraph
lessons	telephone	settled			

Word List 11

dig	hills	filled	it	cities	pits
big	if	in	little	this	milkman
thick	listen	didn't	winter	Kipperville	

Word List 12

stop	jobs	Popperville	got	doctor	top
Bopperville	Kopperville	not	hot	forgotten	rocking

Word List 13

Mulligan	such	dug	cut	trucks	junk
rust	hundred	sun	up	sundown	much

Did you identify the short vowel in each word list? The list below tells the type of phoneme found in each word of the lists.

- List 10—Short *e* phoneme, or /e/, as in *Hester*
- List 11—Short *i* phoneme, or /i/, as in *Jillian*
- List 12—Short *o* phoneme, or /o/, as in *Moppy*
- List 13—Short *u* phoneme: /u/, as in *cut*

The short vowel is very common in children's beginning reading materials, because three letter words, which are easy to recognize and remember, often contain this phoneme. For example, the letter "a" in the word *cat* represents the short vowel sound of "a." Because of this, many teachers teach the short vowel phoneme early in the primary grades, usually in the first grade and sometimes in kindergarten. Again, you can use children's literature characters for associations with these phonemes. Short vowels are listed in Figure ML2.2.

Figure ML2.2 ■ Short Vowel Phoneme Mnemonics

- /a/ as in *cat* from *The Cat in the Hat* (Seuss, 1957)
- /e/ as in *Hester* from *Hester the Jester* (Shecter, 1977)
- /i/ as in *Jillian Jiggs* from *Wonderful Pigs of Jillian Jiggs* (Gilman, 1988)
- /o/ as in *Moppy* from *Mop Top* (Freeman, 1955)
- /u/ as in *Cut-ups* from *The Cut Ups* (Marshall, (1985) or *Gumpy* from *Mr. Gumpy's Outing* (Burningham, 1970)

Figure ML2.3 lists the vowels as they appear in the beginning of words, or the "initial position," as well as in the middle of words, or in the "medial position." The vowels, when in combination with each other and with some consonants, represent many other sounds, but the sounds shown in the chart are the ones most often associated with the letters.

Figure ML2.3 ■ Vowel Sounds as Represented in Words in the Initial and Medial Positions.

Short Vowel Sounds	Long Vowel Sounds
short *a*—/a/ or ă initial position: "apple" medial position: "cat"	long a—/ā/ initial position: "acorn" medial position: "cake"
short *e*—/e/ or ĕ initial position: "eggs" medial position: "jet"	long e—/ē/ initial position: "eagle" medial position: "teeny"
short *i*—/i/ or ĭ initial position: "igloo" medial position: "swim"	long i—/ī/ initial position: "icicle" medial position: "line"
short *o*—/o/ or ŏ initial position: "octagon" medial position: "mop"	long o—/ō/ initial position: "oak" medial position: "rose"
short *u*—u/ or ŭ initial position: "umbrella" medial position: "cut"	long u—/ū/ initial position: "use" medial position: "music"

Self-Quiz for Mini-Lesson 2

1. Test yourself. In each of the following groups, which word does not belong? Explain why.

   a. acorn, able, ate, apple

   b. sight, sin, hide, line

   c. ukulele, unicorn, under, use

   d. peach, pet, read, sneeze

2. In each of the following groups, which word contains a long vowel sound?

   a. pain, have, car, sat

   b. fought, hog, mode, love

   c. eat, when, sieve, egg

   d. hit, height, igloo, itch

3. Test yourself. In each of the following groups, which word does not belong? Explain why.

   a. has, bacon, flat, cask

   b. city, sick, sin, sign

   c. uniform, utmost, but, hug

   d. pest, pen, red, meter

4. In each of the following, which word contains a short vowel?

   a. pain, acorn, car, sat

   b. fine, hog, goat, lake

   c. eat, cheese, eel, egg

   d. height, night, igloo, sky

Review for Mini-Lesson 2

In this lesson, you saw examples of a long vowel phoneme in several words. Each of the vowels, *a, e, i, o, u,* can represent a phoneme that sounds just like the name of the vowel. A word that contains a long vowel phoneme can be spelled in several ways. For example, the words *ate* and *eight* both contain a long *a* vowel phoneme. This phoneme, regardless of how it is spelled, is /ā/.

In the second part of this lesson, you saw examples of the short vowel phoneme in several words. Each of the vowels, *a, e, i, o, u,* can represent a phoneme that has a different sound from the long vowel sound. These phonemes can be spelled in several ways. For example, the words *plaid* and *pad* each contain the short *a* phoneme.

You learned that a good way to remember these phonemes is to associate a word or name with each of the vowels.

Mini-Lesson 3: Y and W as Vowels

Two letters most often associated with consonants can also be considered vowels. Take a look at the following exercises to see how this happens.

The Letter Y. Read the words in Word List 14 taken from *Tacky the Penguin* by Helen Lester (1988). Pay close attention to the last syllable in each word. As you examine these words, ask yourself these questions.

What letter is at the end of each word?

What phoneme do you hear at the end of each word?

Word List 14

tacky	goodly	neatly	lovely	icy	quietly
politely	hearty	splashy	pretty	only	growly
especially	gracefully	loudly	dreadfully	tightly	

You've probably determined that each of these words ends with a *y*, and that the *y* in these words represents the long *e* phoneme, as in *baby*. Thus, the *y* can represent a vowel as well as a consonant. In these words, it is the vowel phoneme /ē/.

Now listen to the vowel phoneme in the words in Word List 15.

Word List 15

shy	my	why	sky

What is the *y* doing here? Each word ends in *y*, which says the vowel phoneme /ī/, as in the words *by* and *hi*. Again, the *y* is a consonant that can also serve as a vowel. Often, when you see it at the end of a word, like in these two lists, it represents either /ē/ or /ī/.

There's another time when *y* serves as a long vowel. Look at Word List 16.

Word List 16

day	away	play	say	may	hey	whey

When the *y* follows the letter *a*, a very consistent pattern occurs. The *y* becomes part of a vowel team, and together with the letter *a*, represents the phoneme /ā/. On occasion, the *y* teams with the letter *e*, to form the team *ey*, as in *hey*. Again, the phoneme is /ā/.

The *y* can also be found in the middle of a word, like in the words *gym*, *myth*, and *gyrate*. When the letter *y* is by itself in the medial position of a word or syllable, it usually represents the phonemes that the letter *i* makes. These phonemes can be either short, as in *gym*, or long, as in *gyrate*.

The Letter *W*.   Let's look at another letter, *w*. In Word List 17, you can see how it serves as part of a vowel team.

Word List 17

new	pew	few	paw	saw	raw
how	cow	sow	tow	row	

In each of these words, the *w* teams with a vowel and the two letters together represent a vowel sound. The usual consonant sound of the *w*, such as /w/ heard in *will*, is not evident. Unlike the *y*, the *w* does not serve as a vowel on its own. It must be in combination with a vowel in order to represent a vowel sound.

Self-Quiz for Mini-Lesson 3

1. Which of the following words does not belong? Why?
   a. my, yellow, sly, skylight
   b. happy, stinky, beyond, funny

2. Which word contains the *y* serving as a vowel?
   a. yonder, why, yippee, yes
   b. yelp, canyon, only, yikes
   c. young, yoke, yank, day

3. In which word is the *w* helping to represent a vowel sound?
   a. wonder, saw, while, way

Review for Mini-Lesson 3

The letter *y* can serve as a vowel. When it is in the final position in the word, it can represent the /ē/ phoneme (as in *baby*), the /ī/ phoneme (as in *my*), or, when teamed with *a* or *e*, the /ā/ phoneme (as in *way* or *hey*). When the letter *y* serves as a vowel in the middle of a word, it represents one of the sounds of *i* (as in *gym* or *rhyme*).

The letter *w* can also serve as a vowel, in words such as *saw, few, how,* and *row*.

Mini-Lesson 4: R-Controlled Vowels

To find out about a special type of vowel phoneme, look at the words in Word List 18, shown below. You can find these words in *Arthur's Reading Race* by Marc Brown (1996).

Word List 18

Arthur   car   park   smart

Each word contains an *a*, but neither the long nor the short sound of *a* is represented. Instead, the phoneme that you should hear is something like the *ar* in *bar*.

Now look at the words in Word List 19 taken from *Charlotte's Web* by E. B. White (1952). Examine them carefully and say them aloud.

Word List 19

Fern   certainly   were   her   person   perfect

Each of these words has a vowel phoneme in common. They have the vowel sound that you hear in the word *herd*. What is it? Look at the words again closely. What do you notice about the placement of the vowel *e* in each word? Do you see the *r*? In each word, the first *e* is followed by an *r*. That makes a big difference in the way that the *e* is pronounced. It is not a long *e* sound, nor is it a short *e* sound. To learn more about this type of vowel phoneme, look carefully at the words in Word Lists 20–23, and then say them aloud.

Word List 20

bird   fir   stir   shirt   skirt   squirm

Word List 21

story   forgotten   gory   horse   forty   corn

Word List 22

church   lurk   turtle   hurt   slurp   cheeseburger

Word List 23

care   air   hair   scare

Each of the words in these lists contains what is called an "r-controlled" vowel phoneme. When a vowel is followed by an *r* in the same syllable, the phoneme that they represent together is not long, nor is it short. It is simply different, and the vowel is considered to be controlled by the *r*, thus, its name. Figure ML4.1 shows these phonemes.

Figure ML4.1 ■ R-Controlled Vowel Sounds

The letters	often represent the phoneme	as in
ar	/ar/	barn
er	/ûr/	fern
ir	/ûr/	bird
or	/or/	corn
ur	/ûr/	church
air	/âr/	hair

Self-Quiz for Mini-Lesson 4

Test yourself.

1. Look at the words below. Replace the final consonant in each of them with an "r." What happens to the vowel phoneme?

   cat   _____

   hem   _____

   fin   _____

   fun   _____

2. Is the vowel phoneme in the word "fort" a short vowel?

3. Is the vowel phoneme in the word "corn" a long vowel?

4. Which of the following words does not contain an r-controlled vowel phoneme? Why?

   work, war, roar, bereave

Review for Mini-Lesson 4

In this lesson, you learned that the placement of the letter *r* affects the vowel phoneme in a word. In most words, when the letter *r* follows a vowel in the same syllable, the phoneme is said to be "r-controlled." Notice the example in number 4 of the self-quiz. Because the *r* was not in the same syllable, it is not part of the vowel phoneme. Thus, *bereave* does not contain an r-controlled vowel phoneme.

Mini-Lesson 5: Vowel Digraphs

Look at Word List 24 and identify how the words are alike. Most of the words are taken from *The Art Lesson* by Tomie DePaola (1989). Look at them closely and say each aloud.

Word List 24

sheets	wait	paint	teacher	boat	Jeannie
green	peel	sleep	cartwheels	though	

Did you notice that each of the words has two vowels together in one syllable? You should also notice that each of the vowel phonemes represented by those pairs of vowels is a long sound. For example, the word *wait* contains a long /a/ phoneme.

Now look at the words in Word List 25, also taken from *The Art Lesson* by Tomie DePaola.

Word List 25

friends   built   too   school   cousins   head   already   could

These words also contain two adjacent vowels in a syllable. However, they are different from the words in Word List 24. They do not contain long vowel sounds. In most, there is a short vowel sound, usually of one of the vowels present in the word. There are many other words that have vowel combinations representing something other than the long sound of the first vowel. Some examples are shown in Word List 26.

Word List 26

book	soot	cough	trough	through	
break	steak	piece	relieve	eight	neighbor

The words shown in each of the lists above contain two adjacent vowels, or a **vowel team.** In each word, this vowel team represents a single phoneme, called a **vowel digraph.** A vowel digraph is a combination of two or three vowels in the same syllable, which represent a single vowel sound. Often, the long vowel sound of one of the letters in the combination is heard (usually the first one), as in the words *meat, sheep, rain, goat, pie.* But this is not always true. Sometimes, the vowel digraph represents the short vowel sound of one of the vowels in the combination, as in the words *cough, rough, head,* and *built.* And sometimes, the vowel digraph represents a vowel sound that is not associated with either of the vowels in the combination, such as in the words *boot, cook,* and *eight.*

Thus, vowel digraphs are complicated teams of letters. Because of the many phoneme possibilities that they represent, vowel digraphs are difficult for many children to decode when they encounter them in unknown words. But learning about them can be made quite simple if you teach them as words that are members of "families," or words that look and sound alike. Mini-Lessons 9 to 12 will show you some spelling patterns that can be helpful.

Self-Quiz for Mini-Lesson 5

1. Which of the following words contains a long vowel?

   mark   goat   bit   sure

2. Which of the following words does NOT contain a vowel digraph?

   sail   sale   eight   steak

3. Which of the following words contains a vowel digraph that represents a long vowel phoneme?

   built   cheap   friend   tough

Review for Mini-Lesson 5

In this lesson you learned that vowels are often combined, representing a variety of phonemes. Two or more vowels together in the same syllable are called a vowel team. Sometimes, a vowel team represents the long sound of the first vowel, such as in the word *dream*. Other times, a vowel team represents the short sound of one of the vowels, such as in the word *head* or *build*. And still other times, the vowel team represents a phoneme not associated with either of the vowels, such as in the word *eight*. When a vowel team represents a single sound, as in all of these examples, the team is called a vowel digraph. A vowel digraph is defined as a combination of vowels (or vowel team) in the same syllable, which represents one sound.

Mini-Lesson 6: Vowel Diphthongs

Now, let's look at some words containing vowel teams that are a little bit different from the ones you saw in Lesson 5. Look carefully at the words shown below. Say them aloud.

Word List 27

cow	how	now	town
couch	found	out	hound

These words also contain vowel teams. The words contain the vowel teams *ow* and *ou*. (Remember the *w* can serve as a vowel, making it a part of the vowel team shown here.) These vowels do not represent long or short vowel sounds. Instead, the sound in each of the words is *ow*, like the sound you would make when you stub your toe!

Look at the words shown below. Say them aloud, too.

Word List 28

boil	coin	toil	join
boy	toy	enjoy	employ

The vowel phoneme in these words is the one that you hear in the word *boy*. (Remember the *y* can serve as a vowel, so that's why it's considered part of this vowel team.) The vowel phoneme in each of these words also is neither long nor short. These two vowel phonemes are special ones, called "gliding vowel sounds," that are unique, blended sounds of these letters. The sound that you make when you pronounce each of these vowel phonemes is one that actually combines two sounds, but is so closely blended that it "glides" right out of the voice box. The term for this type of phoneme is **vowel diphthong.**

Self-Quiz for Mini-Lesson 6

1. Which of the following words contains a vowel diphthong?

    slouch   coach   main   friend

2. Which of the following words contains a vowel digraph?

    boy   street   care   bird

3. Which of the following words contains a vowel diphthong?

    through   though   out   tough

4. Which of the following words does NOT contain a vowel dipthong?

    foam   foil   coin   mountain

Review for Mini-Lesson 6

This lesson introduced the vowel diphthongs, which are vowel teams that represent a gliding sound. The two vowel diphthongs that you learned are the sounds represented by the *ou* in *couch* and the *oi* in *coin*. The letters *ow* and *oy* can also represent the vowel diphthong.

Mini-Lesson 7: Schwa

To find out about yet another type of vowel phoneme, read the words in Word List 29 aloud. Be sure to pronounce them as you normally would.

Word List 29

America   ability   Santa   telephone   captain   Christmas

Notice the length of each of these words. All of them have more than one syllable. Pronounce the words again, making sure to say them as naturally as possible. Find the unaccented syllable in each, and pay attention to the way you pronounce this syllable. See if this syllable sounds like this: "uh." Look at the words below. Which is the unaccented syllable? Which vowel is present in that syllable?

America: _____   Santa: _____   captain: _____

ability: _____   telephone: _____   Christmas: _____

You should have determined that the unaccented syllable in each of the words above contains at least one vowel, and the vowel varies. Sometimes it's an *a*, sometimes it's an *e*, and sometimes it's a vowel team. All of these words have this in common: They are multi-syllable words, and their unaccented syllables, regardless of the vowels that are present, sound like "uh."

This type of phoneme is called a *schwa*. It's the phoneme that is heard in an unaccented syllable of a multi-syllable word, and it can be represented by any vowel, as well as by a combination of letters, as in the second syllable of *table* (/tā/ /bəl/). Phonetically it's represented by the symbol ə, and it sounds like "uh." The schwa sound is often influenced by dialect, and your students' ability to identify the schwa sound "... is not essential to reading success" (Rasinski & Padak, 2001, p. 11). It helps, however, for *you* to know what it is, so that you don't confuse it with other vowel sounds. Additionally, as your students learn dictionary skills, they will encounter the schwa symbol, and you will need to be able to explain what it means.

Self-Quiz for Mini-Lesson 7

1. Which of the following words contains a schwa?

   acorn   bee   appendix   when

2. Which of the following words does NOT contain a schwa?

   agility   button   phoneme   around

3. Which of the following words contains a schwa?

   gun   lost   professional   remake

Review for Mini-Lesson 7

In this lesson, you learned about the schwa phoneme. This is the vowel sound that you hear in the unaccented syllable of multi-syllable words. It is pronounced "uh," and can be represented by any vowel, such as the *a* in *apparent*, or the *i* in *magnify*. The schwa can be also represented by a combination of letters, such as the *-le* in *able* or the *-io* in *nation*. While it is helpful for you to know about it so that you do not confuse it with other vowel sounds, your students' reading ability is not dependent upon knowledge of this term. As they learn to use the dictionary, they will see the ə symbol; thus, you need to be able to define the schwa for them.

Mini-Lesson 8: Hard and Soft C and G

While there are exceptions to generalizations for the consonants *c* and *g*, they occur frequently enough to help with phonetic decoding.

Notice that all of the words in Word List 30 start with *c*. Sometimes, though, the *c* represents the /k/ phoneme, and sometimes, it represents /s/. Can you figure out the conditions under which these sounds are made?

Word List 30

could	called	come	cool
cozy	complain	catch	cup
center	city	citation	cerebrum
civic	Cindy	cents	cereal

In all of the words in the first two rows, the initial phoneme is /k/. In the last two rows, the initial phoneme is /s/. Now, look at the vowels that follow the *c*. In the first two rows, they are all *a, o,* or *u*. In the last two rows, they are *e* or *i*.

What can we generalize from this? When *e* or *i* follow the *c*, it will probably represent the /s/ phoneme, called the "soft" sound of *c*. When the *c* is followed by *a, o,* or *u*, it will probably represent the /k/ phoneme, which is called the "hard" sound of *c*. These are very consistent patterns, with few exceptions.

A similar generalization holds true for the letter *g*. Look at Word List 31.

Word List 31

going	go	got	good
guzzle	gall	gun	game
gentle	giant	gem	gesture
gist	gin	gee	generation

In each of the words in the first two rows of Word List 31, the *g* is followed by *a, o,* or *u*. The sound represented by the grapheme *g* is "hard" phoneme /g/, as in the word *gut*. The generalization you can make here is that when you see a *g* followed by *a, o,* or *u*, it is likely that the *g* will be pronounced like the *g* in *go*.

The words in the last two rows begin with the /j/ phoneme, as in the name *Gina*. You can see that *e* or *i* follows the *g* in each of those words. This is the "soft" sound of *g*. The generalization, which is rather consistent, says that *g* followed by *e* or *i* can safely be pronounced as /j/. However, words that appear to fit the generalization, but do not, are *give, get*, and *girl*. So, while the generalization holds true most of the time, there are some exceptions.

Self-Quiz for Mini-Lesson 8

Test yourself. In each of the following, which word does not belong? Explain why.

1. certain, city, Celeste, candle   _____
2. goofy, ginger, gold, gawk   _____
3. call, cut, cure, circle   _____
4. giggle, generate, gender   _____

Review for Mini-Lesson 8

In this mini-lesson, you learned about the phonemes that are represented on a rather predictable basis by the consonants *c* and *g*.

The grapheme *c*, when followed by an *e* or an *i* in the same syllable, usually represents the /s/ sound, as in *city*. This is called the "soft" sound of the letter *c*. When the *c* is followed by an *a, o,* or *u*, it represents the /k/ sound, as in the word *cot*. This is the "hard" sound of the letter *c*. This generalization is very consistent.

The grapheme *g*, when followed by an *a, o,* or *u* often represents the /g/ sound, as in *got;* this is called the "hard" sound of *g*. The *g* followed by *e* or *i* in the same syllable usually represents the /j/ sound, as in *gentle*. This is called the "soft" sound of the letter *g*. This generalization is also consistent; some exceptions are *girl*, *give*, and *giggle*.

Mini-Lesson 9: The CVC or Closed Syllable Pattern

Patterns of letters in our language are somewhat predictable, and can help the reader determine unfamiliar words. The next generalization is one that is useful for determining the sound represented by the vowel in certain words.

The words in Word List 32 are from *Buz-z-z Said the Bee* by Wendy Lewison (1992). Look carefully at each word and say it aloud. All of these words contain a short vowel. They are also of the same type of spelling pattern. Can you identify the pattern?

Word List 32

sat   hen   pig   jig

Each begins with a consonant, then has a vowel in the middle, and ends with a consonant. This is called the **CVC pattern.** Usually, when you see words like this, you'll hear a short vowel in them. Another name for this pattern is the **closed syllable** pattern.

The words shown in the next list also fit the CVC pattern. Take a look.

Word List 33

duck   scat   cluck   just   fast   then

They, too, contain a short vowel. The only difference is that there is a consonant letter combination either at the beginning or at the end of each word. Those consonants are still part of the CVC pattern. For example, the *ck* in *duck* serves as the final consonant phoneme. Thus, it is still a CVC word.

Multi-syllable words also can contain CVC patterns. Look at the next list.

Word List 34

blister   cobweb   silly   pantry   splendid

As you can see, the CVC pattern is in at least part of each word. For example, the *pan-* in *pantry* begins with a consonant, has the /a/ phoneme in the middle of the word, and ends with a consonant.

Now look at the words in Word List 35 and say them out loud to yourself.

Word List 35

is   us   at   on

These words also contain short vowel phonemes, but they do not begin with a consonant. However, they are still considered words that fit the CVC pattern. The first consonant may be dropped. These words are parts of word families, or **rimes,** for words like *this, bus, hat,* and *Don.* Thus, they are considered words that fit the CVC pattern. Many useful teaching activities for phonics take advantage of the fact that simple words are comprised of rimes, as well as **onsets.** In the CVC word *hat,* the *h* is the onset, and *-at* is the rime. Your students can learn how to remove the onset and replace it with another one, to combine with the rime for a new word. They learn very early that *hat* can be changed to *cat* or *fat* simply by changing the onset.

Self-Quiz for Mini-Lesson 9

1. Which one of the following words fits the CVC pattern?

   mat, mate, car, sign, more   _____

2. Which one of the following words does not belong?

   cab, bit, sun, pen, gold   _____

3. Which one of the following words contains a short vowel?

   hot, home, lonely, ace, far   _____

4. Which one of the following words does not belong?

   tuck, flop, drum, believe, slat   _____

5. What does the CVC generalization state?   _____

_____

Review for Mini-Lesson 9

In this lesson, you became acquainted with some words that fit the CVC pattern, or the closed syllable pattern. This generalization states that words with a vowel between two consonants (in the same syllable) usually have a short vowel phoneme. Words that fit this pattern can also contain consonant combinations, such as in the word *duck*, *drum*, or *clock*. Consonant blends, such as the *ck* in *duck*, or the *dr* in *drum*, are considered to be "consonant units." Consonant digraphs, such as the *th* in *with*, or the *ch* in *chip*, are also considered to be consonant units. Thus, when you see words such as *flop*, *shot*, or *lack*, you may safely assume that these words fit the CVC pattern. The "C" in the acronym "CVC" refers to any consonant or consonant unit.

This generalization includes words that have no beginning consonant, a single vowel, and a final consonant, such as the words *an* and *up*; they, too, usually have short vowel phonemes. You also saw some multi-syllable words that contain this pattern, such as the words *different* and *raccoon*. You can find the CVC pattern in the first syllable of both of these words. According to Clymer (1963, 1996), the CVC generalization holds true in about 62% of words that are found in children's reading materials.

Mini-Lesson 10: The CVCe Pattern

The next set of exercises will help you determine another common generalization that is useful for children to know. Look carefully at the following words shown in Word List 36 and say them aloud. They come from the book, *Seven Blind Mice* by Ed Young (1992).

Word List 36

mice	home	rope	came	side	wide
fine	tale	snake	whole	white	

What kind of vowel is in each? You should hear the long vowel sound, represented by the first vowel in each word. For example, in the word *rope*, you hear the /ō/ phoneme. But you don't hear a phoneme represented by the *e* at the end of the word. These words fit a pattern that is fairly consistent and useful for children to know. It is called the **CVCe** pattern. In words that fit this pattern, the first vowel is often long, and the *e* is silent.

Words like the ones in the list below also fit this pattern. Take a look.

Word List 37

surprise	decide	tolerate	behave	inside	stampede
age	ate	ode	use	ace	

The words in the first row contain the CVCe pattern in the last syllable of the word. This is quite common in multi-syllable words. The words in the second row of Word List 37 also fit, even though they have no beginning consonant. These words all have a long first vowel and a silent *e*. They are parts of word families that fit the CVCe pattern, so they fit, too. Remember, the initial consonant can be missing.

Can you think of a word that looks like it ought to fit this pattern, but doesn't? The word *have* is a word like that. At first glance, it seems to fit, because it looks like a CVCe word. But its first vowel is short, not long. Thus, it is not considered a CVCe pattern word, and is called an "irregularly spelled word."

Self-Quiz for Mini-Lesson 10

1. Which of the following words contains a long vowel phoneme in the middle position?

   take, tab, hat, lost   _____

2. In which of the following words is the *e* silent?

   vet, fern, mile, shell   _____

3. Which of the following words fits the CVCe pattern?

   have, love, give, gave   _____

Review for Mini-Lesson 10

The generalization that you learned in this lesson is called CVCe, the pattern in which the middle vowel represents its long sound and the final *e* is silent. As in the CVC generalization, the initial consonant does not have to be present, such as in the word *ice*. Also, a consonant unit can represent the first phoneme, such as in the words *shake* or *smoke*. According to Clymer (1963, 1996), when the middle vowel is *a* or *i*, this generalization holds true in 60% of the words found in children's reading materials. Some words, such as the word *give*, look as if they fit the pattern, but do not contain a long medial vowel. Therefore, they are considered to be "irregularly spelled" words.

Mini-Lesson 11: The CVVC Pattern

The generalization presented in this lesson is one that is perhaps the most misunderstood, yet it is quite a useful one to know. Read the words in Word List 38, which were taken from *Green Eggs and Ham* by Dr. Seuss (1960).

Word List 38

green   train   rain   goat   boat

How do all the words in Word List 38 look alike? You should see that each contains a vowel team. And what type of vowel phoneme do you hear in each word?

The long phoneme is present in each of the words in this list. And, you'll notice that all of the words look similar, in that they all begin and end with consonants and have the vowel team in the middle. The acronym for this pattern is **CVVC**. This generalization says that when there are adjacent vowels in the middle of a word, the first vowel is long and the second one is silent.

Clymer (1963, 1996) found this generalization to be true in 45% of the words in children's reading materials. The frequency rate increases for specific vowel combinations, such as *ai* (64%), *ea* (66%), and *oa* (97%). Historically, this pattern has often been taught as a "phonics rule" in classrooms; however, Clymer determined that its utility rate does not justify teaching it as a rule. (You may remember the "rule," which states, "When two vowels go walking, the first one does the talking.") With a 45% utility rate, there are too many words in which the vowel combination does not represent the long sound of the first one for this to be considered a "rule."

Is it worth learning as a generalization? I contend it is, because it gives the young reader one tool for figuring out an unknown word – one that will work almost half the time when encountering a difficult word. That certainly narrows down the choices and gives the reader a good chance of decoding the vowel phoneme. So, be aware of this generalization, but also be aware that there are many other possible phonemes associated with vowel combinations.

Recall from Mini-Lesson 5 that a vowel digraph is a combination of two adjacent vowels, within a syllable, which represents a single vowel sound. The words *built*, *friend*, and *float* all contain a vowel digraph, because there is only one vowel sound in each of these words, represented by a pair of vowels. However, the word *float* is the only one that fits the CVVC pattern, because it is the only one in which the first vowel is long and the second one is silent. Thus, remember that all CVVC words contain vowel digraphs; however, not all vowel digraphs fit the CVVC pattern.

Self-Quiz for Mini-Lesson 11

1. Which of the following words contains a long vowel phoneme?

   train, mad, loft, his   _____

2. Which of the following words fits the CVVC pattern?

   head, piece, like, boat   _____

3. Which of the following words does not belong in this list?

   mail, sleep, hat, road   _____

4. What can be said of words that "fit" the CVVC pattern?

_____

5. Which of the following words contains a long vowel phoneme, according to the CVVC pattern?

growl, bead, bike, cousin   _____

Review for Mini-Lesson 11

In this lesson you learned of a special type of vowel digraph, the CVVC pattern. In words that fit this pattern, the first vowel is long and the second one is silent. According to Clymer (1963, 1996), this generalization or pattern "works" in 45% of words that have two adjacent vowels in the same syllable. Thus, some words that contain vowel digraphs look like they should fit the pattern, such as *book*, *head*, *sail*, and *belief*. However, these words do not follow the generalization because the first vowel in each of these words is not long. Words like *main*, *float*, and *heat* contain vowel digraphs that do fit the CVVC pattern. This pattern is useful for children to know, because it gives them a starting place for decoding unknown words with vowel teams. If a student sees an unfamiliar word with two adjacent vowels and does not recognize a word family in the word, he or she would be well-advised to try the long sound of the first vowel and see if that produces a word that makes sense.

Mini-Lesson 12: The CV or Open Syllable Pattern

Even though the next generalization applies to words that are just two letters long, it is extremely helpful for determining vowel phonemes in longer words. Read on to find out how. Examine the words in Word List 39. Look at their spellings, then say them aloud.

Word List 39

me   be   no   we   he   my

Do you hear a long vowel phoneme in all of these words? Remember, the *y* can serve as a vowel, and in this case, it represents the /ī/ sound.

Look at the words shown in Word List 40. They are similar to the ones in List 39. Say them aloud.

Word List 40

bacon   November   rehabilitation   station

Now, each of these words contains the same type of pattern that you saw in List 39. The difference is that these words are longer, containing multiple syllables. But you can find little parts within these big words, and they look like the words in List 39.

The acronym for this pattern is **CV**. This means that a word that fits this pattern contains a long vowel phoneme, the one represented by the vowel that you see in the word. For example, in the word *be*, you hear the long /e/ phoneme. This is also called an **open syllable.** An open syllable contains a long vowel, and there is no consonant on the end of the word or syllable.

Now say the words in Word List 41 aloud.

Word List 41

I   A   acorn   April   even   over

You'll notice that a long vowel is also represented in each of these words. The difference in these words, though, is that there is no beginning consonant. However, they still fit this pattern. The first consonant in the CV pattern is dropped.

But look at Word List 42. They are also a bit different.

Word List 42

to   do   who

How do these words compare to the words in the first three lists of this lesson? You can't hear a long vowel phoneme in these. Thus, they look as if they fit the CV pattern, but they don't, because the long vowel is not present. They are called irregularly spelled words.

Self-Quiz for Mini-Lesson 12

1. Which of the following words contains a long vowel phoneme?

   he, to, can, some _____

2. Which of the following words fits the CV pattern? How do you know?

   do, spa, me, car _____

3. Which of the following words does not belong on this list? Why?

   my, be, is, we _____

4. Which of the following words contains the CV pattern? How do you know?

   token, spaghetti, lung, eggs _____

5. Which of the following words is irregularly spelled? How do you know?

   toe, dive, why, to _____

Review for Mini-Lesson 12

In Lesson 12, you saw what happens in words or syllables that contain a single vowel with no consonant at the end. In many words, when there is a single consonant (or consonant unit) followed by a single vowel, the vowel phoneme is long. Such is the case in the words *me* and *my*. (Remember, *y* can be considered a vowel.) This is the CV pattern; also called an open syllable. This pattern also holds true for many words or syllables that consist of only one vowel, such as the word *I* and the first syllable of the word *acorn*. (In those cases, the acronym is "V.") Clymer (1963, 1996) says that this generalization holds true for 74% of the words in children's reading materials.

Sometimes, however, the generalization does not hold true, even though the word looks as if it might. For example, in the word *ability*, most people pronounce the first syllable with an "uh" sound, not a long *a* sound. In cases like this, the vowel phoneme is a schwa sound. As you will recall, the schwa is a vowel phoneme that says "uh," and it occurs only in multi-syllable words, in the unaccented syllable of the word.

There are other words that look like a CV pattern but don't contain the long vowel phoneme, such as the word *do*. This is called an irregularly spelled word because it is not pronounced according to the predictable patterns based on its appearance.

Mini-Lesson 13: Syllabication Patterns

When readers encounter an unfamiliar multi-syllable word, their ability to break it apart into manageable pieces will facilitate successful decoding. Thus, it is important to know some simple patterns that help when deciding how to break a word into syllables for pronunciation.

Closed Syllable.   Look at Word List 43. These words are taken from *Cook-a-Doodle-Doo!* (Stevens & Crummel, 1999). I have divided the first syllable from the second one in each of the words.

Word List 43

hungry: hun-gry	butter: but-ter	granny: gran-ny
fluffy: fluf-fy	funny: fun-ny	into: in-to
until: un-til	under: un-der	mixture: mix-ture
picture: pic-ture	better: bet-ter	ingredients: in-gredients
center: cen-ter	magnificent: mag-nificent	

What do you notice about each of these words? There are two important commonalities. Say each word to yourself again. Notice that the first syllable of each word has a short vowel. That is the first important common attribute. The second important attribute is that the first syllable in each word ends with a consonant. This is a common pattern and can help readers figure out where to divide a long word into manageable pieces and how to pronounce the results. It is the closed syllable, introduced in Mini-Lesson 9. Closed syllables end in a consonant and the vowel just prior to the consonant is often short.

Open Syllable.   Word List 44 shows another syllabication pattern. You'll find these words in *Dandelions* (Bunting, 1995b). Again, they have been divided into syllables. See if you can determine the pattern.

Word List 44

baby: ba-by	behind: be-hind	below: be-low
china: chi-na	pretend: pre-tend	silence: si-lence

What type of vowel sound do you hear in the first syllable of each word? Where is each word divided? You should have determined that each of these words is pronounced with the long vowel in the first syllable, and that each word is divided after the first vowel.

This type of syllabication pattern is called the open syllable, which you learned about in Mini-Lesson 12. Open syllables end in a single vowel, which is often long.

It is important to know, however, that many words can confuse the reader. For example, if the student is unfamiliar with the word *metal* and divides it after the first vowel, as taught in the pattern you see above, the student would pronounce it as *mee-tul*. Since it should be pronounced as *mĕt-ul*, it is important to teach the student to always do a self-check and put the word in a sentence. The important self-question to ask is, "Does this pronunciation make sense in this sentence?"

-le words. A third common syllabication pattern that will be helpful is shown in Word List 45.

Word List 45

table: ta-ble	stable: sta-ble	possible: pos-si-ble
beetle: bee-tle	scramble: scram-ble	

Notice how the last syllable of each of these words ends in the *le,* plus its preceding consonant. The last syllable in each rhymes with *full.* This is a very consistent pattern. Thus, when your students see an unfamiliar word that ends in the *le* combination, they can safely assume that the last syllable consists of the *le* plus the preceding consonant. They can divide the word just prior to that, and determine the phonemes in those syllables using familiar patterns.

Self-Quiz for Mini-Lesson 13

Divide the words shown below and indicate the vowel sound in the first syllable.

1. belly   _____
2. lady   _____
3. clover   _____
4. potpie   _____
5. amber   _____
6. able   _____
7. nimble   _____
8. tremble   _____
9. candle   _____
10. hassle   _____

Review for Mini-Lesson 13

In this lesson, you learned three common syllabication patterns. The first, called the closed syllable, consists of a short vowel followed by a consonant, as in the words *batter* and *center.* The second pattern you learned is the open syllable, in which the syllable ends in a long vowel. Examples are *bacon, silent,* and *Susan.* The third pattern discussed in this lesson is the one associated with words that end in *-le.* The pattern in these words is to include the consonant prior to the *-le* in the syllable, as in *cable* (ca-ble), *thimble* (thim-ble), and *tussle* (tus-sle). You also learned that some words look as if they fit the open syllable pattern, but they do not. An example of such a word is *second.* The student who is unfamiliar with this word would not know how to divide the word and pronounce it. He or she may think that it contains an open syllable, and pronounce it like this: "sē-cond." In actuality, it contains the closed syllable: "sĕc-ond." The reader must check this by asking, "Does this word make sense in this sentence?"

Mini-Lesson 14: Words with Affixes

To see how easy words with affixes can be, take a look at Word List 46. These words are from *In a People House* (LeSieg, 1972). What do you notice about all of the words?

Word List 46

chairs	skates	bottles	brooms
rooms	buttons	doughnuts	peanuts

Suffixes.   You probably noticed right away that they all end in the letter *s*. Each of the words is a noun, and the *s* ending indicates that the noun is plural, or more than one. This is the most common type of word ending, or suffix. It is an inflectional suffix because it does not alter the meaning of the word; rather, it changes the number of the word, or makes it plural. This suffix is the most common in children's printed materials (White, Sowell, & Yanagihara, 1989). Its "sister" suffix is *-es*, which is shown in Word List 47. This list shows words that end in the phonemes /s/, /sh/, or /ch/. When making these words plural, the *-es* must be added.

Word List 47

beaches	boxes	churches	matches	dishes	dresses

Additionally, you have seen words like the ones in Word List 48.

Word List 46

parties	bellies	babies	ladies
pennies	dragonflies	butterflies	stories

These are words whose roots ended in *y*. When the *-es* is added to the word, the *y* must be changed to *i*.

You probably also know another way that *-s* is used on words. Look at Word List 49. What do you notice?

Word List 49

reads	messes	dives	dresses	plays	teaches
helps	reaches	stands	fusses	jumps	belches
sits	wishes				

All of these words are verbs. The *-s* or *-es* must be added to verbs, to indicate agreement with number, such as in this sentence: The woman _____ everyday. To add the verb *walk* to this sentence, and have it make sense in English, *-s* needs to be added, to make the word *walks*. To add the word *teach*, the *-es* must be added.

Knowing about this affix and its meanings is highly useful, because 31% of the words in children's reading materials that have suffixes end in either *-s* or *-es* (White, Sowell, & Yanagihara, 1989).

The next three most common suffixes are shown in Word List 50. All of these words can be found in Dr. Seuss's "The Sneetches" from *The Sneetches and Other Stories* (1961). Take a look at them and think about what you know.

Word List 50

roared	fixing	quickly
clambered	wishing	actually
jerked	paying	precisely
worked	screaming	nicely
groaned	walking	frightfully
yelled	talking	really
frowned	moping	exactly
packed	doping	perfectly
laughed	sitting	probably
treated	running	
opened	working	
announced	changing	
guaranteed		
removed		
invited		
zipped		

These word endings are probably quite familiar to you. The first column consists of verbs that are in past tense; thus, the *-ed* has been added to the root words. Sometimes, because the word already ends in the letter *e,* the only addition to the word is the letter *d,* such as in the word *invited.* Other times, the final consonant in the word needs to be doubled before adding the *-ed,* such as in the word *zipped.*

The second column is a list of words that are very common in our language. These words are verbs that end in the *-ing* suffix, and *-ing* indicates the present participle. The *-ing* can also be used to indicate the result of some verb, such as in the word *painting.* A sentence that illustrates this is: "Someone who paints produces a painting."

The third column is a list of words ending in *–ly.* A common usage of this suffix is to indicate how something is done. Such a word is an adverb, like the word *nicely.* According to White, Sowell, and Yanagihara (1989), these three suffixes account for about 72% of the affixed words that your students will read. Knowledge of them is quite helpful in building vocabularies.

Look at Word List 51 for still another common suffix. All of these words appear in *Maybe You Should Fly a Jet! Maybe You Should Be a Vet!* (LeSieg, 1980).

Word List 51

taker	maker	fixer	dancer	mixer	jailer	nailer
wrestler	writer	waiter	forester	miner	designer	hanger
plumber	owner	loaner	smeller	teller	farmer	teacher
preacher	framer	tamer	walker	talker	diver	actor
grower	blower	tuner	doodler	sculptor	jester	tester

As you can see, the commonality in these words is the *-er* or *-or* suffix. These word endings change a verb to a noun, in that the new word is someone who does the action indicated in the verb. For example, the verb *act* becomes *actor*, which means "someone who acts." Approximately 4% of the suffixes that your students will see are of this type.

The sixth most common type of suffix, and its various spellings, is shown in Word List 52.

Word List 52

pollution	education	confusion	prohibition
election	medication	explosion	demolition
collection	explanation	permission	
eruption	hibernation		
	fascination		
	identification		

The *-ion* suffix, and its spelling variations, often indicate that the root word, a verb, was changed to a noun. Doing something (the verb) results in a thing that was done (the noun). Thus, to use an example, if people "pollute" the air, the result is "pollution." In another example, if I "confuse" my students, the result is "confusion," but if I "educate" them, the happy result is "education."

Speaking of confusion, this word ending can create just that. Look at the words in the next Word List.

Word List 53

faction	friction	mission
compassion	condition	nation

While these words end with "-ion" or one of its spelling variants, the meaning of the word is not indicated by a combination of root word and suffix. For example, the word *nation* does not mean a "na" that results in a "nation."

Prefixes. What about word parts that are attached to the beginnings of words? These are called prefixes, and Word List 54 shows examples of the top six, according to White, Sowell, and Yanagihara (1989).

Word List 54

unhappy	reread	inaccurate	discomfort	enable	nonliving
unclean	rewrite	inability	disable	enforce	nonmember
unhurt	repaint	inappropriate	discolor	enlarge	nonreader
unsafe	rewash	inexpensive	disfavor	enjoy	nonfiction
untamed	remarry	impossible	disfigure	empower	nonpaying
unworn	reexamine	impolite	dislike	embattle	nonworking
		immature			
		irrational			
		irresponsible			
		illegal			

Your familiarity with these words can help you figure out the meanings of the prefixes. What can you tell about each of the prefixes shown above? Answer the questions below.

How does the prefix *un-* change the word *happy*? _____

How does the prefix *re-* change the word *write*? _____

How does the prefix *in-* change the word *accurate*? _____

How does the prefix *im-* change the word *polite*? _____

How does the prefix *ir-* change the word *responsible*? _____

How does the prefix *il-* change the word *legal*? _____

How does the prefix *dis-* change the word *comfort*? _____

How does the prefix *en-* change the word *able*? _____

How does the prefix *non-* change the word *living*? _____

You probably realized that if you know that *unhappy* means "not happy," you can make an assumption that *unsafe* means "not safe." While this happens a lot, it is not always true. There are some prefixes that Cunningham calls "unpeelable," which means that the word is not recognizable when the prefix is "peeled off" (2005, p. 144). An example of this is the word *expire*. Taking off the *ex-* from this word produces *pire*, which is not a word and does not have meaning on its own.

Additionally, prefixes can have multiple meanings. For example, the prefix "un-" means "not" in words like *unsafe* and *unhurt*. But it means "do the opposite" in the words *untie* and *undo*. Moreover, the same meaning can be represented by several prefixes, which are usually spelled very similarly. For example, in the third column of Word List 54, you can see the words *irresponsible*, *impossible*, and *illegal*. All of these prefixes mean *opposite*.

Mini-Lesson 14 covers a lot of ground. See how well you remember all of this by taking the Self-Quiz.

Self-Quiz for Mini-Lesson 14

1. Which is the most common suffix in children's reading materials? _____

2. In what two ways are the suffixes *-s* and *-es* used?

   a. _____

   b. _____

3. What does the suffix *-ed* usually mean when added to a root word?

   _____

4. Which of the following words contains a suffix?   flying   swing   wing

5. How does the suffix *-ly* change the word *nice*?

   _____

6. How does the suffix *-er* change the word "dance?"

   _____

7. What does the addition of the suffix *-ion* (and its spelling variations) do to root words such as *collect*, *explode*, and *identify*?

   _____

8. Write a brief definition of the following words:
   a. unharmed   _____
   b. reevaluate   _____
   c. insecure   _____
   d. immobile   _____
   e. disorganized _____
   f. envision   _____
   g. nonacademic   _____

Review for Mini-Lesson 14

In this lesson, you learned about affixes, which are word parts added to the ends of words (suffixes), and word parts that are attached to the beginnings of words (prefixes).

Inflectional suffixes do not alter the meaning of the word, such as in the word *books*. The *-s* ending indicates a change in number for the word "book," but the meaning of "book" remains the same. The most common word ending is the *-s*. It can indicate plurality, or it can indicate noun-verb agreement, such as in the word *reads*. Additionally, the *-s* ending changes the spelling of some words, such as *beach*, the plural of which is spelled *beaches*, or *party*, the plural of which is *parties*.

Two more common inflectional suffixes are *-ed*, which indicates past tense (as in *laughed*), and *-ing*, which indicates the present participle form of verbs (as in *talking*). Other common suffixes change the meanings of words. Two of these are the *-ly*, which usually changes an adjective into an adverb (as in *quickly*), and the *-er* or *-or* suffix, which changes a verb to a noun, in that the new word is someone who does the action indicated in the verb (as in *teacher*).

You also learned that the *-ion* suffix, and its spelling variations, often indicate that the root word, a verb, such as *educate*, has changed to a noun, such as *education*. Sometimes students get confused because not all word endings are suffixes, such as the *-ion* in *mission*.

Prefixes are attached to the beginnings of words. The top six, according to White, Sowell, and Yanagihara (1989) are *un-*, *re-*, *in-*, *dis-*, *en-*, and *non-*. However, there are some prefixes that Cunningham calls "unpeelable," which means that the word is not recognized when the prefix is "peeled off" (2005, p. 144). An example of this is the word *expire*. Taking off the *ex* from this word produces *pire*, which is not a word and does not have a meaning on its own, Additionally, some prefixes have multiple meanings.

Answer Key to Self-Quizzes

Mini-Lesson 1

1. thing—The other two words begin with consonant blends.

2. spin—The other two words begin with consonant digraphs.

3. shot—The other two words begin with consonant blends.

4. this—The other two words begin with a silent consonant.

5. night—The other two words contain consonant blends. "Night" contains silent consonants.

6. that—The other two words begin with consonant blends. In the word "shrug," the *sh* represents a phoneme of its own, and the *r* represents a phoneme of its own. Thus, the two consonant phonemes are blended.

7. tough—The *gh* combination in each of the other two words is silent.

Mini-Lesson 2

1. a. apple (The *a* in each of the other words represents the long vowel.)

   b. sin (The *i* in each of the other words represents the long vowel.)

   c. under (The *u* in each of the other words represents the long vowel.)

   d. pet (the *e* in each of the other words represents the long vowel.)

2. a. pain
   b. mode
   c. eat
   d. height

3. a. bacon (It is the only word with the long *a*.)
   b. sign (It's the only word with the long *i*.)
   c. uniform (It's the only word with the long *u*.)
   d. meter (It's the only word with the long *e*.)

4. a. sat
   b. hog
   c. egg
   d. igloo

Mini-Lesson 3

1. a. yellow—The *y* represents a consonant phoneme in this word. The *y* in the other words on the list represents the vowel phoneme.

   b. beyond—The *y* represents a consonant phoneme in this word. The *y* in the other words on the list represents the vowel phoneme.

2. a. why
   b. only
   c. day

3. a. saw

Mini-Lesson 4

1. car, her, fir, fur (These vowel phonemes all changed from short vowels to r-controlled ones.)

2. no

3. no

4. bereave – The *r* starts the second syllable; therefore, it's not part of the vowel phoneme in the first syllable.

Mini-Lesson 5

1. goat
2. sale
3. cheap

Mini-Lesson 6

1. slouch
2. street
3. out
4. foam

Mini-Lesson 7

1. appendix
2. phoneme
3. professional

Mini-Lesson 8

1. "Candle," because it does not have an initial /s/ phoneme, as in the rest of the words on the list.

2. "Ginger," because it does not have an initial /g/ phoneme, as in the rest of the words on the list.

3. "Circle," because it does not have an initial /k/ phoneme, as in the rest of the words on the list.

4. "Giggle," because it does not have an initial /j/ phoneme, as in the rest of the words on the list. It is an exception to the generalization. In most cases, a *g* followed by an *i* would represent /j/.

Mini-Lesson 9

1. mat
2. gold
3. hot
4. believe
5. When there is a consonant unit at the beginning of the word or syllable, followed by a single vowel, with a consonant unit at the end of the word or syllable, it is likely that the vowel sound will be short.

Mini-Lesson 10

1. take
2. mile
3. gave

Mini-Lesson 11

1. train
2. boat
3. hat
4. The vowel phoneme is the long sound of the first one.
5. bead

Mini-Lesson 12

1. he
2. me—It contains the long *e* phoneme.
3. is—The other words fit the CV pattern, "is" does not.
4. token—the *o* is long
5. to—This is irregularly spelled because the *o* is not long.

Mini-Lesson 13

1. bĕl-ly
2. lā-dy
3. clō-ver
4. pŏt-pie
5. ăm-ber
6. ā-ble
7. nĭm-ble
8. trĕm-ble
9. căn-dle
10. hăs-sle

Mini-Lesson 14

1. The most common suffix in children's reading materials is -*s*.

2. a. to indicate plurality in nouns (such as in *cats*)

   b. to indicate noun-verb agreement (such as in "The girl reads.")

3. The suffix -*ed* usually means that the verb is past tense.

4. flying

5. The suffix -*ly* changes the adjective "nice," which describes a noun, to an adverb, "nicely," which describes a verb.

6. The suffix -*er* changes the verb "dance" to a noun, "dancer," which means "someone who dances."

7. These verbs become nouns that indicate the result of the verbs. For example, when you collect, you now have a collection.

8. a. unharmed—*not harmed*

   b. reevaluate—*evaluate again*

   c. insecure—*not secure*

   d. immobile—*not mobile*

   e. disorganized—*not organized*

   f. envision—*to have a vision or picture*

   g. nonacademic—*not academic*

References

Allington, R., (2001). *What really matters for struggling readers: Designing research-based programs.* New York: Longman.

Allington, R. (2005, June/July). The other five "pillars" of effective reading instruction. *Reading Today, 22* (6), 3.

Alvermann, D., Moon, J., & Hagood, M. (1999). *Popular culture in the classroom: Teaching and researching critical media literacy.* Newark, DE: International Reading Association.

Anderson, R. C. (2004). Role of the reader's schema in comprehension, learning, and memory. In R. Ruddell, & N. Unrau. (Eds.), *Theoretical models and processes of reading* (5th ed., pp. 594–606). Newark, DE: International Reading Association.

Anderson, R. C., & Pearson, P. D. (1984). A schema-theoretic view of basic processes in reading comprehension. In P. D. Pearson (Ed.), *Handbook of reading research* (pp. 255–291). New York: Longman.

Antonacci, P. & O'Callaghan, C. (2006). *A handbook for literacy: Instructional and assessment strategies K–8.* Boston: Allyn & Bacon.

Bednarz, S., Miyares, I., Schug, M., & White, C. (2003). *World cultures and geography.* Evanston, IL: McDougal Littell.

Berks County Intermediate Unit (2000). K–12 benchmarks: Language arts. Retrieved August 3, 2005, from http://www.berksiu.k12.pa.us/.

Block, C. (2004). *Teaching comprehension: The comprehension process approach.* Boston: Allyn & Bacon.

Calkins, L. (2001). *The art of teaching reading.* New York: Longman.

Calkins, L., Montgomery, K., Santman, D., & Falk, B. (1998). *A teacher's guide to standardized reading tests.* Portsmouth, NH: Heinemann.

Cohen, J., & Wiener, R. (2003). *Literacy portfolios: Improvement assessment, teaching, and learning.* Upper Saddle River, NJ: Merrill Prentice Hall.

Clay, M. (1985). *The early detection of reading difficulties* (3rd ed.). Portsmouth, NH: Heinemann.

Clay, M. (2000). *Running records for classroom teachers.* Portsmouth, NH: Heinemann.

Clay, M. (2005). *An observation survey of early literacy achievement* (2nd ed.). Auckland, New Zealand: Heinemann.

Clymer, T. (1963). The utility of phonic generalizations in the primary grades. *The Reading Teacher, 16,* 252–258.

Clymer, T. (1996). The utility of phonic generalizations in the primary grades (RT Classics). *The Reading Teacher, 50*(3), 182–187.

Cunningham, P. (2005). *Phonics they use* (4th ed.) Boston: Pearson/Allyn & Bacon.

Cunningham, P., & Cunningham, J. (1992). Making words: Enhancing the invented spelling-decoding connection. *The Reading Teacher, 46*(2), 106–115.

Cunningham, P., Hall, D. & Defee, M. (1991). Nonability grouped, multilevel instruction: A year in a first grade classroom. *The Reading Teacher, 44*(8), 566–571.

Cunningham, P., Hall, D., & Defee, M. (1998). Nonability-grouped multilevel instruction: Eight years later, *The Reading Teacher, 51*(8), 652–664.

Cunningham, P., Moore, S., Cunningham, J., & Moore, D. (2000). *Reading and writing in elementary classrooms (4th Ed.).* New York: Longman.

Dreher, M. J. (2002). Children searching and using informational text. In C. Block, & M. Pressely (Eds.), *Comprehension instruction: Research-based best practices,* pp. 289–304. New York: Guilford Press.

Duke, N., & Pearson, P. D. (2002). Effective practices for developing reading comprehension. In A. Farstrup, & S. Samuels (Eds.), *What research has to say about reading instruction* (3rd ed., pp. 205–242). Newark, DE: International Reading Association.

Eldredge, J. L. (2004). *Phonics for teachers: Self-instruction, methods, and activities.* Upper Saddle River, NJ: Pearson.

Fountas, I., & Pinnell, G. S. (2001). *Guiding readers and writers grades 3–6: Teaching comprehension, genre, and content literacy.* Portsmouth, NH: Heinemann.

Glazer, S. (1998). *Assessment is instruction: Reading, writing, spelling, and phonics for all learners.* Norwood, MA: Christopher Gordon.

Goldman, S. R., & Rakestraw, J. A. (2000). Structural aspects of constructing meaning from text. In M. Kamil, P. Mosenthal, P. D. Pearson, & R. Barr (Eds.), *Handbook of reading research* (Vol. 3, pp. 311–335.) Mahwah, NJ: Lawrence Erlbaum.

Goodman, Y., & Goodman, K. (2004). To err is human: Learning about language processes by analyzing miscues. In R. Ruddell, & N. Unrau, (Eds.). *Theoretical models and processes of reading* (5th ed., pp. 620–639). Newark, DE: International Reading Association.

Harris, T., & Hodges, R. (1995). *The literacy dictionary: The vocabulary of reading and writing..* Newark, DE: International Reading Association.

Harvey, S., & Goudvis, A. (2000). *Strategies that work: Teaching comprehension to enhance understanding.* Portland, ME: Stenhouse.

Johns, J., & Bergland, R. (2002). *Fluency: Questions, answers, evidence-based strategies.* Dubuque, Iowa: Kendall/Hunt Publishing.

Kagan, S. (1994). *Cooperative learning.* San Clemente: Resources for Teachers.

Kletzien, S. & Dreher, M. (2004). *Informational text in k–3 classrooms: Helping children read and write.* Newark, DE: International Reading Association.

Leslie, L., & Caldwell, J. (1990). *Qualitative reading inventory.* NY: HarperCollins.

Leu, D. (2002). The new literacies: Research in reading instruction with the Internet. In A. Farstrup, & S. J. Samuels (Eds.), *What research has to say about reading instruction* (3rd ed.), pp. 310–336. Newark, DE: International Reading Association.

Martin-Kniep, G. O. (2003). Using standards-based portfolios and other assessment tools to promote curriculum goals. In J. Cohen, & R. Wiener (Eds.), *Literacy portfolio: Improving assessment, teaching, and learning* (pp. 183–200). Upper Saddle River, NJ: Merrill Prentice Hall.

Morrow, L. M. (1991). Promoting voluntary reading. In J. Jensen, D. Lapp, J. Flood, & J. Squire (Eds.), *Handbook of research on teaching the English language arts* (pp. 681–690). New York: Macmillan.

Moss, P. (2004). Teaching expository text structures through information trade book retellings. *The Reading Teacher, 57*(8), 710–718.

National Reading Panel. (2000). *Teaching children to read: An evidence-based assessment of the scientific research literature on reading and its implications for reading instruction.* (NIH Publication No. 00–4769). Washington, D.C.: National Institute of Child Health and Human Development.

Nettles, D. (2006). *Comprehensive literacy instruction in today's classrooms: The whole, the parts, and the heart.* Boston: Allyn & Bacon.

Opitz, M. & Rasinski, T. (1998). *Goodbye, round robin: Twenty five effective oral reading strategies.* Portsmouth, NH: Heinemann.

Palincsar, A., & Brown, A. (1984). Reciprocal teaching of comprehension-fostering and comprehension-monitoring activities. *Cognition and Instruction, 1,* 117–175.

Palmer, R. G., & Stewart, R. (2003). Nonfiction tradebook use in primary grades. *The Reading Teacher, 57*(1), 38–47.

Pennsyvlania Department of Education. (1999). *Academic standards for reading, writing, speaking and listening.* Retrieved April 11, 2006 from http://www.pde.state.pa.us/k12/lib/k12/reading.pdf.

Pressley, M., Levin, J., & Delaney, H. D. (1982). The mnemonic keyword method. *Review of Educational Research, 52*(1), 61–91.

Rasinski, T., & Padak, N. (2001). *From phonics to fluency: Effective teaching of decoding and reading fluency in the elementary school.* New York: Addison Wesley Longman.

Rosenblatt, L. (1978). *The reader, the text, and the poem: The transactional theory of the literary work.* Carbondale: Southern Illinois University Press.

Routman, R. (2000). *Conversations: Strategies for teaching, learning, evaluating.* Portsmouth, NH: Heinemann.

Routman, R. (2003). *Reading essentials: The specifics you need to teach reading well.* Portsmouth, NH: Heinemann.

Rumelhart, D. (1980). Schemata: The building blocks of cognition. In R. Shapiro, B. Bruce, & W. Brewer (Eds.), *Theoretical issues in reading comprehension* (pp. 33–8). Hillsdale, NJ: Erlbaum.

Sadoski, M., & Paivio, A. (2004). A dual coding theoretical model of reading. In R. Ruddell, & N. Unrau (Eds.). *Theoretical models and processes of reading* (5th ed., pp. 1329–1362.) Newark, DE: International Reading Association.

Samuels, S. J. (2002). Reading fluency: Its development and assessment. In A. Farstrup & S. J. Samuels (Eds.), *What research has to say about reading instruction* (3rd ed., pp. 166–183). Newark, DE: International Reading Association.

Samuels, S. J. (2004). Toward a theory of automatic information processing in reading, revisited. In R. Ruddell, & N. Unrau (Eds.), *Theoretical models and processes of reading* (5th ed., pp. 1127–1148). Newark, DE: International Reading Association.

Schwartz, R., & Raphael, T. (1985). Concept of definition: A key to improving students' vocabulary. *The Reading Teacher, 39*(2), 198–205.

Schmitt, M. (1990). A questionnaire to measure children's awareness of strategic reading processes. *Reading Teacher, 43*(7), 454–461.

Shanahan, T. (2003). Research-based reading instruction: Myths about the National Reading Panel report. *The Reading Teacher, 56*(7), 646–655.

Shanker, J. & Ekwall, E. (2000). *Ekwall/Shanker reading inventory.* Boston: Allyn and Bacon.

Spandel, V. (2001). *Creating writers through six trait writing assessment and instruction.* New York: Addison Wesley Longman.

Villaume, S. K., & Brabham, E. G. (2001). Guided reading: Who is in the driver's seat? *The Reading Teacher, 55*(3), 260–263.

Watson, G. (1996). *Teacher smart!* West Nyack, NY: The Center for Applied Research in Education.

The White House. (2006). Harry S Truman. Retrieved April 18, 2006, from http://www.whitehouse.gov/history/presidents/htm33.html.

White, T. G., Sowell, J., & Yanagihara, A. (1989). Teaching elementary students to use word-part clues. *The Reading Teacher, 42*(4), 302–308.

Williams, J. P. (1993). Comprehension of students with and without learning disabilities: Identification of narrative themes and idiosyncratic text representations. *Journal of Educational Psychology, 85*(4), 631–641.

Yaden, D., Rowe, D., & MacGillivray, L. (2000). Emergent literacy: A matter (polyphony) of perspectives. In M. Kamil, P. Mosenthal, P. D. Pearson, & R. Barr, *Handbook of reading research: Volume 3* (pp. 425–454). Mahwah, NJ: Lawrence Erlbaum.

Yahooligans. (1996). Yahooligans! The web guide for kids. Retrieved April 8, 2006, from http://yahooligans.yahoo.com.

Children's Literature References

Alvarez, J. (2002). *Before we were free.* New York: Alfred Knopf/Random House.

Arnosky, J. (2002). *All about frogs.* New York: Scholastic Press.

Avi. (2001). *The secret school.* Orlando, FL: Harcourt.

Babbit, N. (1975). *Tuck everlasting.* New York: Farrar, Straus, & Giroux.

Bierhorst, J. (2001). *Is my friend at home? Pueblo firesde tales.* New York: Farrar, Straus, & Giroux.

Blume, J. (2002). *Double Fudge.* New York: Scholastic.

Blume, J. (1971). *Freckle juice.* New York: Bantam Doubleday.

Bourgeois, P. (2001). *Oma's quilt.* Toronto: Kids Can Press.

Brown, M. (1986). *Arthur's teacher trouble.* New York: Scholastic.

Brown, M. (1991). *Arthur meets the president.* Boston: Joy Street/Little, Brown & Co.

Brown, M. (1996). *Arthur's reading race.* New York: Random House.

Bunting, E. (1995a). *Cheyenne again.* New York: Clarion.

Bunting, E. (1995b). *Dandelions.* San Diego: Voyager/Harcourt.

Bunting, E. (1998). *So far from the sea.* New York: Clarion.

Bunting, E. (2001). *Gleam and glow.* San Diego: Harcourt.

Burningham, J. (1970). *Mr. Gumpy's outing.* New York: Henry Holt.

Burton, V. L. (1939). *Mike Mulligan and his steam shovel.* Boston: Houghton Mifflin.

Choi, N. S. (1991). *Year of impossible goodbyes.* New York: Dell.

Choi, Y. (2001). *The name jar.* New York: Alfred Knopf.

Cleary, B. (1965). *The mouse and the motorcycle.* New York: William Morrow.

Cleary, B. (1981). *Ramona Quimby, age 8.* New York: Scholastic.

Clements, A. (1996). *Frindle.* New York: Simon & Schuster.

Codell, E. R. (2003). *Sahara special.* New York: Scholastic.

Cole, J. (1986). *This is the place for me.* New York: Scholastic.

Curtis, C. P. (1999). *Bud, not Buddy.* New York: Scholastic.

Dahl, R. (1961). *James and the giant peach.* New York: Penguin.

deGroat, D. (2000). *Jingle bells, homework smells.* New York: HarperCollins.

dePaola, T. (1989). *The art lesson.* New York: Putnam.

dePaola, T. (1993). *Tom.* New York: Putnam & Grosset.

Diaz, J. (1993). *The rebellious alphabet.* New York: Henry Holt.

DiCamillo, K. (2000). *Because of Winn-Dixie.* Cambridge, MA: Candlewick Press.

Dorris, M. (1992). *Morning girl.* New York: Hyperion Children's Books.

Finchler, J. (2000). *Testing Miss Malarkey.* New York: Walker Publishing.

Freeman, D. (1955). *Mop top.* New York: Puffin Books.

Galdone, P. (1984). *The teeny-tiny woman.* New York: Clarion.

Gerstein, M. (2003). *The man who walked between the towers.* Brookfield, CT: Roaring Brook Press.

Giff, P. R. (1984). *The beast in Ms. Rooney's room.* New York: Dell.

Gilman, P. (1988). *The wonderful pigs of Jillian Jiggs.* Toronto: Scholastic Canada.

Henkes, K. (1991). *Chrysanthemum.* New York: Trumpet.

Hennessey, B. G. (1990). *Jake baked the cake.* New York: Viking.

Hill, E. (1987). *Spot's first picnic.* New York: Putnam's Sons.

Hoffman, M. (1991). *Amazing Grace.* New York: Dial.

Hoffman, M. (2002). *The color of home.* New York: Phyllis Fogelman Books/Penguin Putnam.

Holliday, L. (1999). *Why do they hate me? Young lives caught in war and conflict.* New York: Pocket Books.

Houston, G. (1992). *My great-aunt Arizona.* New York: HarperCollins.

Hutchins, P. (1968). *Rosie's walk.* New York: Aladdin Paperbacks.

Ibbotson, E. (2004). *The star of Kazan.* New York: E. P. Dutton.

Johnson, A. (1992). *The leaving morning.* New York: Orchard Books.

Konigsburg, E. L. (2000). *Silent to the bone.* New York: Simon and Schuster.

Koss, A. (2003). *The cheat.* New York: Dial.

LeSieg, T. (1972). *In a people house.* New York: Random House.

LeSieg, T. (1980). *Maybe you should fly a jet! Maybe you should be a vet!* New York: Random House.

Lester, H. (1988). *Tacky the penguin.* New York: Trumpet.

Lewison, W. C. (1992). *Buzzz said the bee.* New York: Scholastic Cartwheel.

Lindgren, A. (1997). *Adventures of Pippi Longstocking.* New York: Viking.

Lionni, L. (1968). *The alphabet tree.* New York: Trumpet.

Lionni, L. (1963). *Swimmy.* New York: Pantheon Books.

Lobel, A. (1980). *Fables.* New York: Harper & Row.

Lobel, A. (1976). *Frog and Toad all year.* New York: Harper Trophy.

Lowry, L. (1993). *The giver.* New York: Bantam Doubleday Dell.

Lowry, L. (2002). *Gooney Bird Greene.* Boston: Houghton Mifflin.

Marshall, J. (1984). *George and Martha back in town.* Boston: Houghton Mifflin.

Marshall, J. (1985). *The cut-ups.* New York: Viking.

McCloskey, R. (1941). *Make way for ducklings.* New York: Viking.

McGovern, A. (1967). *Too much noise.* Boston: Houghton Mifflin.

Millman, I. (2000). *Moses goes to school.* New York: Farrar, Straus, & Giroux.

Nagda, A. W. (2000). *Dear whiskers.* New York: Holiday House.

Parish, P. (1981). *Amelia Bedelia and the baby.* New York: Avon.

Paterson, K. (1977). *Bridge to Terabithia.* New York: HarperCollins.

Paulsen, G. (1996). *Brian's winter.* New York: DelaCorte Press.

Polacco, P. (1994). *Pink and Say.* New York: Philomel Books.

Polacco, P. (1998). *Thank you, Mr. Falker.* New York: Philomel Books.

Polacco, P. (2000). *The butterfly.* New York: Philomel Books.

Potter, B. (1987). *The tale of Peter Rabbit* (Reissue edition). New York: Scholastic.

Radunsky, V. (2004). *The mighty asparagus.* San Diego, CA: Silverwhistle/Harcourt.

Recorvits, H. (2003). *My name is Yoon.* New York: Frances Foster Books/Farra, Straus, & Giroux.

Ryan, P. M. (2000). *Esperanza rising.* New York: Scholastic.

Sachar, L. (1998). *Holes.* New York: Farrar, Straux, & Giroux.

Schotter, R. (1999). *Nothing ever happens on 90th street.* New York: Orchard Books.

Scieszka, J. (1991). *The frog prince continued.* New York: Penguin.

Segal, L. (1977). *Tell me a Trudy.* New York: Farrar, Straus, & Giroux.

Sendak, M. (1963). *Where the wild things are.* New York: Scholastic.

Seuss, Dr. (1940). *Horton hatches the egg.* New York: Random House.

Seuss, Dr. (1957). *The cat in the hat.* New York: Random House.

Seuss, Dr. (1960). *Green eggs and ham.* New York: Random House.

Seuss, Dr. (1961). *The Sneetches and other stories.* New York: Random House.

Shecter, B. (1977). *Hester the jester.* New York: Harper & Row.

Simon, S. (1989). *Whales.* New York: HarperCollins.

Simon, S. (2001). *Animals nobody loves.* New York: Scholastic.

Soto, G. (1996). *The old man and his door.* New York: Putnam & Grosset.

Soto, G. (1993). *Too many tamales.* New York: G. P. Putnam's Sons.

Spinelli, J. (2000). *Stargirl.* New York: Knopf.

Steig, W. (1969). *Sylvester and the magic pebble.* New York: Simon and Schuster.

Stevens, J. (1995). *Tops and bottoms.* New York: Scholastic.

Stevens, J. & Crummel, S. (1999). *Cook-a-doodle-doo!* Orlando: Harcourt Brace.

Tolan, S. (2002). *Surviving the Applewhites.* New York: Scholastic.

Uchida, Y. (1981). *A jar of dreams.* New York: Aladdin.

Uegaki, C. (2003). *Suki's kimono.* Toronto, Ontario: Kids Can Press.

Waber, B. (1972). *Ira sleeps over.* Boston: Houghton Mifflin.

Wallace, B. (1980). *A dog called Kitty.* New York: Simon & Schuster.

White, E. B. (1952). *Charlotte's web.* New York: HarperCollins.

Williams, L. (1986). *The little old lady who was not afraid of anything.* New York: Harper-Collins.

Wiseman, B. (1959). *Morris the moose.* New York: HarperCollins.

Yorinks, A. (1986). *Hey, Al.* New York: Sunburst.

Young, E. (1992). *Seven blind mice.* New York: Scholastic.